Distribution Management

Fifth Edition

By

Thomas E. DeCarlo, Ph.D.
University of Alabama at Birmingham

ABOUT THE AUTHOR

Thomas E. DeCarlo is the Ben S. Weil Endowed Chair of Industrial Distribution and Professor of Marketing and Industrial Distribution at the University of Alabama at Birmingham. He has taught in executive MBA programs in China (Beijing, Chongqing), Iowa State University, and the University of Georgia and has been recognized for his outstanding teaching and business impact on several occasions. Dr. DeCarlo has also conducted many seminars and research projects dealing with new product development, market analysis and segmentation, sales force and brand management for companies such as 3M, Agenta Biotechnologies, Lockheed Martin, Andersen Windows, Vermeer Manufacturing, among others. His primary research interests deal with strategic issues in sales force management, customer relationship management, and marketing communications. Dr. DeCarlo's research has been published in journals such as, *Journal of Marketing, Journal of Consumer Psychology, Journal of the Academy of Marketing Science, Journal of Personal Selling and Sales Management, Journal of International Business Studies, Journal of Service Research, and Industrial Marketing Management*. He earned his Ph.D. from the University of Georgia.

Copyright © 2016 by Thomas E. DeCarlo

All rights reserved. No part of this publication may be reproduced, distributed, or transmitted in any form or by any means, including photocopying, recording, or other electronic or mechanical methods, without the prior written permission of the author, except in the case of brief quotations embodied in critical reviews and certain other noncommercial uses permitted by copyright law.

TABLE OF CONTENTS

1	Introduction to Supply Chains and the Role of the Distributor	1
2	Understanding the Value of the Middleman	13
3	Creating and Managing Successful Supplier Relationships	20
4	Distributor Demand Forecasting	35
5	Distributor Operations and Channel Management	51
6	Essentials of Distributor Pricing & Profitability	67
7	Ethical Decision Making and the Distributor	72
8	Account Relationship Management in the Channel of Distribution	93
9	Marketing Promotions in Distribution Channels	118

INTRODUCTION TO SUPPLY CHAINS AND THE ROLE OF THE DISTRIBUTOR

LEARNING OBJECTIVES

After studying this chapter, you should be able to:

- Explain supply chains and the role of distributors.
- Understand how different supplier tiers operate in a supply chain.
- Explain the bullwhip effect.
- Understand disintermediation and why distributors add value in the supply chain.
- Explain the general categories of business markets.

WHAT IS A SUPPLY CHAIN AND HOW DO DISTRIBUTORS PLAY A ROLE?

The terms "supply chain" or "marketing channel" are typically used to describe a set of interdependent organizations that are involved in the process of making a product or service available for use or consumption. In its broadest form, a supply chain includes any activity needed to transfer goods from raw material extraction through consumption by the final consumer. In many channels, a *focal firm* will coordinate the selection of the channel members similar to that of a conductor coordinating the activities of an orchestra. The focal firm often selects suppliers, manufactures or builds the product, and interfaces with the final consumer. However, to be a focal firm does not require an ability or willingness to take on all aspects of managing the product from manufacturing to the final consumer. Johnson and Johnson (J&J), for example, has no manufacturing activities in some of its health care markets, yet is considered the focal firm in those markets because of its dominant brands. There are also supply chains where the focal firm does not sell directly to the consumer. For example, many B2B markets often contract with independent distributors to market their products for them. OSRAM Sylvania, for instance, prefers to let independent distributors market its lighting products to builders and contractors in the construction market rather than sell directly into those markets.

Distributors play a vital role in the supply chain and, in some situations, are considered the focal firm due to their sheer dominance in a particular market. By definition, a distributor is an independent company that purchases and assumes title from the products it purchases and resells them to users and original equipment manufacturers (OEM's). In one sense, managing a distribution branch is similar to owning your own business. The branch manager would select the assortment of brands and products to purchase for resell, manage supplier relationships, maintain adequate inventory stock levels, develop go-to-market strategies, manage all aspects of the sales process and provide customer service. It is important to note that distributors typically do *not* manufacture products; they buy products in basically the same form and resell them to their customers. As we will discuss in more detail throughout this book, they also provide a vast array of value added services in the supply chain for both the manufacturer and customer. If a distributor were unable or unwilling to provide these value added services, there would be little need for them in the marketing channel.

SUPPLIER TIERS

A supply chain also includes the companies that provide the raw products to a manufacturer. An OEM purchases industrial products to build into other products it sells in the business or consumer market. Automobile manufacturers, for example, are typically considered OEMs in the auto industry. The companies that are direct suppliers to OEMs are known as tier one suppliers. Gentex Mirror, for example, is a tier one supplier of high tech rear view mirrors to automobile manufacturers. Tier two suppliers provide product to tier one suppliers; they typically do not sell their products directly to OEM companies. It is also possible for a supplier to be a tier one supplier to one company, but a tier two supplier to another company in the same product line. As you might guess, tier three suppliers provide products to tier two firms. Essentially, the higher the tier level, the farther removed the supplier is from the OEM. Distributors can be any tier in the supply chain, but are most frequently used as tier one suppliers by OEMs.

The categories of OEM or user are not mutually exclusive and are based on the intended purpose the product serves for the customer. GM, for example, would be considered a user when purchasing a machine tool for the manufacturing process, but the same company is an OEM when purchasing seats to be installed in the cars the company builds. Thus, an effective B2B marketer, which includes distributors, should have a good understanding of the diverse organizational consumers that make up the business market. Properly classifying commercial customers as users or OEMs is an important first step to a sharpened understanding of the buying criteria that a particular commercial customer uses in evaluating an industrial product.

The supply chain also includes companies that move the products, such as shipping, railroading, and trucking companies, as well as any warehouses where items may be temporarily stored during movements within the various tiers in the supply chain. Activities involved in managing the movement of materials and components from point to point in the supply chain are referred to as logistics. We will discuss in subsequent chapters how distributors will use logistics as a key strategic advantage in the supply chain.

INFORMATION SHARING AND THE BULLWHIP EFFECT

Information about future demand is a key component in avoiding problems among the various tiers in the supply chain. Unfortunately, some adjacent supply chain pairs might only share limited or no market information because the firms tend to focus on the current or upcoming transaction and do not consider the bigger picture. For example, an OEM might order a certain quantity of units from a distributor, informing the distributor only of the number of units desired at the time and when the units should be delivered. In this instance, virtually no information about expected future changes in demand have been shared between the OEM and distributor. Or if future purchases are shared by the OEM, it might only be limited to the distributor and not shared with other tier one and tier two suppliers. A limited approach to information sharing does not optimize supply chain performance and can even lead to more severe problems that could affect all channel members. One such detrimental effect is called the "bullwhip effect".

THE BULLWHIP EFFECT

The bullwhip effect refers to situations when the demand order variabilities in the supply chain are amplified as they move up the chain (i.e., from OEM to distributor, tier one, tier two, etc.). This effect is caused when product demand information is not fully shared in a supply chain or when updated forecasts are not communicated. The problem is further complicated by combining orders that concentrate demand at one point in time, or using price changes that change demand and/or by one firm in the channel that is just trying to game the system. The bullwhip effect occurs when an OEM or retailer experiences a slight increase in demand and subsequently increases its order quantity to avoid running out of the product. The distributor picks up on the increased order from its customer (the OEM) and, to also avoid running out, it increases its order from its suppliers by a larger amount to ensure it has enough safety stock. The supplier will, in response, increase its orders to its suppliers by a larger amount, again to ensure it has enough safety stock. The end result is that a small increase at the OEM (or retail) level increases nearly exponentially throughout the supply chain, resulting in a large demand increase farther back in the channel. When the OEM places the *next* order, which is similar to its prior (i.e., more normal) orders, each member of the channel will now have too much inventory. In extreme bullwhip situations, a supplier may be forced to lay off employees because the demand can be met from existing inventory. The other firms will see the reduced orders (as compared to the previous order) and will drastically cut production. This scenario is played out often in many supply chains with suppliers at the end of the chain being "whipped" from one extreme to the other, from high demand requiring overtime costs to low demand leading to layoffs or excess inventory. Unfortunately, both of these options increase the supplier's costs.

Is there a way to avoid the bullwhip effect? Keep in mind that the bullwhip cycle typically begins when one company is provided sequential order information at one point in time. Therefore, many companies find that the most effective method in avoiding the bullwhip effect is to share information in real-time about supply and demand among the different companies in the distribution channel. One way to do this is for all members of the supply chain to transmit their forecasts to a central hub with each member having access to the information. The focal firm often determines the information that must be shared in this manner. The reason for sharing this information is that all supply chain partners would be able to see changes occurring anywhere in the supply chain and respond to those changes accordingly without overreacting. *Electronic data interchange (EDI)* is a method of exchanging relevant information between suppliers and customers in real time. *Collaborative planning, forecasting*, and replenishment (CPFR) goes beyond the exchange of data to include joint planning efforts. These concepts, including the bullwhip effect, will be discussed in more detail in subsequent chapters.

SERVICE OPERATIONS

Supply chain management often becomes synonymous with manufacturing because people typically think about it as moving goods from point to point in the production process. However, the supply chain functions of logistics, inventory, and purchasing are important topics in service operations. Health care, for example, is a service business where supply chains and supply chain management are important to both the service provider and the patient. From a traditional supply chain perspective, a hospital has suppliers who provide food, linens, medicine, equipment, and maintenance services for its facilities. Well-run health care organizations also have patients, doctors, hospital clinical staff *and* suppliers exchanging information and working together to understand problems and develop solutions, or novel treatments. This is a highly interactive process where value is created by all of the participants. It is based on trust, commitment and a shared vision that patient welfare is the first priority. In fact, sometimes a trusted supplier may not have the best product for a particular situation and may need to bring in a competing supplier to provide the necessary service for the most positive patient outcome. While these same elements are important in a traditional manufacturing supply chain, they literally could mean life or death in the health care supply chain. Thus, one advantage to purchasing from distributors over manufacturers is they are able to provide a customer with the most appropriate product for a particular need because they typically stock competing brands in a product category; a manufacturer sales rep would only have one brand to market.

DISINTERMEDIATION AND WHY DISTRIBUTORS ADD VALUE TO THE SUPPLY CHAIN

For our purposes, an intermediary is a business entity, such as a distributor, that exists between a manufacturer and a customer. For example, auto dealers are intermediaries between the automobile manufacturers and the customers who buy cars. Some industries attempt to achieve efficiencies in the supply chain by eliminating intermediaries and selling direct to consumers. This is known as disintermediation. Tesla Motors, an automotive manufacturer and energy storage company, sells its autos directly to customers, bypassing the traditional independent dealership channel model. While this distribution model limits the company's ability to have an extensive dealer network, it allows Tesla to maintain direct control over the sales process and service quality. The music industry is another example of disintermediation. Long gone are the days where purchasing an entire album was required to own a favorite song. iTunes and other online music distributors have made it easy to own a single music track. One unfortunate byproduct is that the majority of record stores have gone the way of the dinosaur, or in business terms, they were disintermediated.

Distributors have not only avoided being disintermediated, but, in many markets, have grown in their influence and power in the supply chain. This is is due to at least three reasons: 1. The explosion of information technology and e-commerce; 2. Manufacturer difficulty in gaining a sustainable competitive advantage with price, product, and promotion elements of the marketing mix; and 3. Expanding power of intermediates that have direct contact with customers (i.e., possess customer and market information). We now discuss each in more detail.

Information technology and e-commerce have also fundamentally changed customers' behaviors and expectations and created new demands that must be met to attract and keep customers. In particular, convenience and ease of doing business are becoming critically important for today's B2B customer. What this means is that customers are requiring higher service levels from their suppliers because their customers are demanding increases in product availability, speed of delivery, lower shipping costs, and flexible return policies. Meeting these enhanced customer expectations, particularly when they involve complex products, requires a tremendous amount of attention and resources by a supplier which makes it even more difficult for a manufacturer to focus on both product innovations and production efficiencies as well as meeting these expanding customer demands. Thus, many manufacturers are realizing that it is better to focus on what they do best, which is manufacturing products, and outsource the demand generation and customer fulfillment activities to distributors.

Manufacturers are also finding that achieving a long-term competitive advantage in product innovations, price, or promotion is difficult to maintain, but that place (or distribution) is an area where they can gain a competitive advantage. Product innovations, for example, can be relatively short-lived due to competitive firms' ability to re-engineer any innovative product with a similar product. Recall when Apple revolutionized cellular communication when it introduced the iPhone. The competition quickly introduced products similar to the iPhone and reduced Apple's gains in the marketplace. Price advantages are also not sustainable for building a long-term competitive advantage since some competing firms can withstand lower margins over an extended period of time in an effort to match or beat rival price advantages. Promotions can provide an advantage in the marketplace, but these are not sustainable over the long run since they are oriented toward short-lived gains in sales. In addition, promotions can be prohibitively expensive over time. In terms of place (or distribution channel), many manufacturers have realized that partnering with a distribution firm that has an excellent reputation for outstanding customer service in the marketplace is very difficult to replicate. For example, Mayer Electric, a regionally based electrical distributor in Birmingham, Alabama enjoys a high level of channel equity with its customers, which has been built over decades of being customer focused. Channel equity refers to the value of a supplier's current and future offerings from a particular distributor versus other local distributors. It would be very expensive for a manufacturer to establish and maintain the level of channel equity Mayer provides by selling direct. Many manufacturers, therefore, have realized that using an established distribution channel would lower overall channel costs due to the cost savings of developing and maintaining a competitive marketing and selling program.

Finally, market knowledge and understanding is gained through direct contact with customers. This is particularly important in B2B markets that offer complex products and services. In fact, research unequivocally supports the notion that harnessing a customer knowledge-based competence will yield a competitive advantage in the marketplace because the knowledge gained from customer-specific interactions enables firms to develop customer-specific strategies for effectively engaging prospective and current customers.[1] Thus, distributors are uniquely positioned to gain power and influence in the channel by acquiring and disseminating market and customer knowledge by not only understanding customer needs and wants, but also their underlying motivations.

We now turn to discussing the unique features of business-to-business markets. While there are a few commonalities between the consumer and business markets, B2B buyers and markets function quite differently in many respects, therefore they merit separate attention. For example, business and consumer markets differ in the market demand, buyer behavior, buyer-seller relationships, environmental influences (economic, political, legal), and market strategy. Understanding these differences provides unique challenges and opportunities that can result in high potential payoffs for those distributors and manufacturers that can successfully penetrate their selected business market.

---

[1] Li, T., & Calantone, R. J. (1998, October). The impact of market knowledge competence on new product advantage: Conceptualization and empirical examination. *Journal of Marketing*, 62, 13–29.

Business Markets

The dollar volume of transactions in the industrial or business market significantly exceeds that of the consumer market. In fact, wholesale distribution was a $5.1 trillion industry in 2013.[2] To put this in perspective, the wholesale distribution market represented over 30% of the total U.S. gross domestic product output in 2013.[3] Also, individual firms in business markets can account for a significant level of purchasing activity. For example, the corporate procurement departments of IBM and Apple spend billions annually on industrial products and services. In fact, all business organizations – large or small, public or private, for-profit or not-for-profit – participate in the exchange of industrial products and services, which, in total, comprise the business market.

The business market is broadly defined and includes all transactions except those dealing with products or services directed at personal use or consumption such as home appliances, consumer banking, or grocery products. As noted earlier, business firms purchase industrial goods to facilitate a production process or to use as components for other goods to maintain and deliver services to their own market. It is also important to note that, because of the size of the industrial or business markets, more than 50 percent of all business school graduates join firms that compete directly in the business market.

The customers of business markets can be generally classified into three categories – commercial firms, institutions, and governments. Each of these three markets has identifiable and unique characteristics that must be understood to successfully compete (see Table 1). In fact, a key first step in creating a successful go-to-market strategy is to identify the unique dimensions of each major business market sector. For example, understanding the market potential and how purchase decisions are made would provide a base-line foundation for formulating a marketing strategy of each business market sector. We will limit our discussion in this chapter to an overview of institutional and government sectors. The remaining chapters of

---

[2] 2014 Wholesale Industry Landscape Report, Gale Media Report, retrieved from http://www.mdm.com/ext/resources/MarketLeaders/2014-Market-Leaders/2014-Landscape-Report/Wholesale-Distribution-Landscape-Report-SAMPLE.pdf, July 23, 2015.
[3] Retrieved from http://www.statista.com/statistics/263591/gross-domestic-product-gdp-of-the-united-states/ on July 23, 2015.

Introduction to Supply Chains

this book (and course) focus on the commercial markets and customers in much more detail and will not be discussed here.

Table 1   Types of Business Market Customers

Commercial Customers	**Institutional Customers**	**Governmental Customers**
Manufacturers Construction companies Service firms Transportation companies Selected professional groups Distributors/Wholesalers Retailers	Schools, colleges, universities Health-care organizations Libraries Foundations Art galleries Clinics	Federal government • Non-defense • Defense State government Local government • Counties • Townships

Government Units

Federal (1), state (50), and local (89,000) government units generate the greatest volume of purchases of any single customer category in the United States. Government units purchase from virtually every category of goods and services — office supplies, computers, food, health care, military equipment. The government uses two general purchasing strategies: 1. An open bid process using formal advertising, or 2. A negotiated contract. In open bids, the government solicits proposals from appropriate suppliers. The government typically uses an open bid program when buying standardized products with straightforward specifications, such as laptop computers. Contracts are generally awarded to the lowest bidder; however, the government agency may select the next-to-lowest bidder if it can document that the lowest bidder would not fulfill the contract responsibly.

Negotiated contracts are often used to purchase products and services that are not easily differentiated on the basis of price alone (such as complex scientific research and development equipment) or when there are few potential suppliers. The government develops competition by conducting simultaneous negotiations with competing suppliers. The ultimate purchasing decision is very similar to that of large corporations: Which is the best possible product at the lowest price, and will the product meet performance expectations?

Institutions

Institutional customers comprise the third sector of the business market (see Table 1). Schools and health-care organizations make up a sizable component of the institutional market, which also includes colleges and universities, libraries, foundations, art galleries, and clinics. Many institutional buyers are similar to governments in that the purchasing process is often constrained by legal and political considerations. However, other institutions are privately operated and managed like corporations; they may even have a broader range of purchase requirements than their large corporate counterparts. Similar to commercial enterprises, institutions are adopting sophisticated approaches to purchasing.

Business-to-business marketing and sales personnel should understand the needs and personal characteristics of all participants in the buying process when formulating marketing and personal selling approaches. For example, many university institutional buying groups are staffed with professionals, including doctors, professors, and researchers. Depending on its size, the institution may employ a purchasing agent and, in large institutions, a sizable purchasing department. Often, the salesperson must carefully cultivate the professional staff in terms of product and cost benefits, while developing a delivery timetable, maintenance contract, and price schedule to satisfy the purchasing department. Leading business marketers also use the Internet to provide added value to their customers. For example, Cardinal Health, Inc. a large distributor of medical products, has embraced the Internet as the centerpiece of its marketing strategy and provides an online catalog, daily Internet specials, and a host of services for its customers — purchasing managers at hospitals and health-care facilities worldwide.

Institutional buying often involves group-purchasing associations. Hospitals, schools, and universities will join cooperative purchasing associations in order to secure volume purchasing efficiencies which include lower prices, improved quality (through improved testing and supplier selection), reduced administrative costs, and greater competition. Thus, suppliers need to be equipped to not only respond to the needs of individual institutions, but also be prepared to meet the requirements of cooperative purchasing groups and large hospital chains.

Summary

In this chapter, we began by defining a supply chain as including any activity needed to transfer goods from raw material extraction through consumption by the final consumer. The distributor has a vital role in the supply chain as it represents a $5 trillion industry. The companies that provide materials to a manufacturer are known as tier one suppliers. Tier two suppliers provide products to tier one suppliers and tier three suppliers provide products to tier two suppliers. When demand and supply information is not shared among the various tiers, there is the possibility that the supply chain could experience the bullwhip effect. The bullwhip effect refers to situations when the demand order variabilities in the supply chain are amplified as they move up the chain (i.e., from OEM to distributor, tier one, tier two, etc.). This effect is caused when demand information is not fully shared in a supply chain or when updated forecasts are not communicated. The chapter also discussed the fact that supply chain management is not only about the movement of products, but it also includes important service operations. When a channel member does not provide value to the supply chain, there is a possibility that it would be disintermediated. The trend that distributors are growing in power and influence in the channel is due to at least three reasons: 1. The explosion of information technology and e-commerce; 2. Manufacturer difficulty in gaining a sustainable competitive advantage with price, product, and promotion elements of the marketing mix; and 3. Expanding power of intermediates that have direct contact with customers (i.e., possess customer and market information). The chapter concludes with a discussion of business markets, which are classified into three general categories – commercial firms, institutions, and governments.

Understanding the Value of the "Middleman"

Thomas Craig sunk back into his first class seat as the 747 took off. The perks of flying with the CEO weren't bad, but he knew that there was no such thing as a free lunch. He would soon be meeting with an industrial distribution company that wanted to market and sell their new line of vascular products. Thomas was officially the vice president of research and development at Agenta Biotechnologies, a manufacturer of medical equipment. Unofficially, Thomas was CEO's Bob Roberts' troubleshooter. He called him in on all tough product development questions, but never did he ask for Thomas's opinion on product distribution issues. This was definitely outside of Thomas' expertise. They were flying to the distributor's offices for a meeting to determine if a partnership with the distributorship is a good idea.

After a few minutes in the air, Bob started to talk about the upcoming meeting; "I hope you don't mind coming with me to this meeting, Thomas. We need to make sure that the industrial distributor route is the way we want to go with our vascular product line and I value your opinion."

"Thanks Bob," replied Thomas, "but I don't really have much expertise in the distribution of our products, I just help build them. In fact, I don't even know how an industrial distributor would be better for our company than just selling the vascular products ourselves."

"That's a good question," replied Bob. "Industrial distributors are independent businesses that buy goods from manufacturers like us and sell them to industrial users and sometimes to other resellers. We'll have to see what happens in our meeting, but traditionally, industrial distributors provide six basic functions for manufacturers like us. They make sales contacts, provide market coverage, hold inventory, process orders, gather market information, and provide customer support."

"Really," exclaimed Thomas, "I had no idea that industrial distributors performed all of those functions. How can they do all of those things better than we can?"

"Let me start from the beginning," said Bob. "In terms of making *sales contacts* for manufacturers, the distributor has a number of advantages. First, you need to understand that manufacturers like us are good at making things, but we are not very good at selling and we don't have the expertise or the financial resources to manage a large sales force. This is typical of many mid-sized manufacturers. The reason is that the costs of setting up a sales operation are enormous; an office must be rented and equipped with all the necessary communication and data-processing equipment, staff must be recruited and trained, delivery trucks need to be purchased, additional warehouse space would be needed, the products must be marketed, and the potential customer base has to be identified. A distributor, on the other hand, has the entire infrastructure in place with an established customer base so it is able to provide us sales revenue quickly.

Distributors also provide *market coverage* to manufacturers because our customers, which are hospitals and clinics, are spread out all over the country. To have good market coverage so that our products are available to the doctors when needed, manufacturers like us often rely on independent distributors to represent their products to the market at a reasonable cost. Distributors are uniquely capable of meeting shorter lead times when customers order frequently. I would bet that we would go broke having to deal with different lead times from our end users.

So, as you might imagine, another important task performed by distributors is that they *hold inventory* for manufacturers. The distributor we'll be negotiating with will take title to, and stock our vascular products. In fact, they hold the inventory for all the manufacturers they represent. This reduces our financial burden and reduces some of our risk associated with holding large inventories. It also helps manufacturers to be in a better situation to plan our production schedules by providing a ready outlet for our products. In other words, we won't be as affected by small variations in market demand, the distributor has to deal with that.

As I mentioned earlier, a distributor also helps manufacturers by processing orders. Many customers like to buy in small quantities and manufacturers find it extremely inefficient to attempt to fill a large amount of small orders from thousands of customers. Distributors are specifically geared to handle small orders from many customers. The

Understanding the Value of the Middleman

reason why they can do that is because distributors carry products from many manufacturers which affords them the opportunity to spread the processing costs over a larger array of products. For us to process and fill many small orders would be very expensive. We've actually run the numbers and you would be surprised how much it would cost just to establish one new customer account to process one order. The distributor can do that much cheaper than we can."

Bob continued, "Distributors also *gather market information* for manufacturers like us because they are quite close to their customers geographically and have continuous contact through frequent sales calls. They are uniquely qualified to learn about customers' product and service requirements, which can then be passed on to us manufacturers for future product planning, pricing, and marketing strategies.

Finally, *customer service* is where distributors really play a big role for us. Their salespeople will help individual doctors understand how the product works. In fact, they will even be in the operating room standing next to the doctor during an operation, which is a big benefit for us. Distributors will help exchange, or return, repair, or provide other technical assistance so we don't have to. For manufacturers like us to perform these services directly to all our customers can be very expensive. Instead of dealing with these potential headaches, distributors will carry out these services to our customers."

"OK, I think I understand how they provide value for us, but what value do distributors offer to our customers? I mean, wouldn't hospitals want to buy directly from us?" asked Thomas.

"I knew you were going to ask that question," Bob replied. "Distributors provide all sorts of benefits for customers, but I'll give you the *Reader's Digest* version and talk about the six most important to us. First, they assure *product availability,* which is perhaps the most basic task they perform for customers. Because of the closeness of distributors to our customers and their sensitivity to customers' needs, they can provide a level of product availability that many manufacturers couldn't easily match.

Second, a distributor provides *credit and financial assistance* for customers. There are a couple of ways they can do this. The first way is by extending open account credit to customers so that doctors can use our products in the hospital or clinic before having to pay for them. It's up to the distributor to run a credit check and offer credit – something we don't want to touch with a ten-foot pole. A second way is by keeping stock for customers and having the stock ready when they need it. By doing this, distributors reduce the financial inventory burden of their customers since they don't have to purchase and stock all of the products themselves.

Third, distributors offer *assortment convenience* by bringing together from a variety of manufacturers a wide variety of products that greatly simplifies customers' ordering tasks. Similar to buying all of your groceries from one grocery store instead of going to the butcher, baker and bread maker for your food, a hospital can turn to one general-line distributor to provide them with most or all of the products they need. This saves hospital personnel a tremendous amount of time and expense."

"As you probably already know," Bob continued, "hospitals and clinics require services such as on-time delivery, repairs, or warranty work. All of these *customer service* activities are considered essential for distributors to survive in the market – which is the fourth customer benefit. By providing these services, as well as offering prompt, professional service, distributors provide peace of mind for hospital administrators. As you can see, if we took on these tasks we wouldn't have any time to invent new products."

"I can certainly see how my time would be chewed up with putting out customer service fires," offered Thomas.

"I know, they can offer a lot of customer value," responded Bob. In fact, one of the biggest values that they offer is their *breaking bulk* function. "

"OK, you got me, what does 'breaking bulk' mean?" asked Thomas.

"Well," Bob continued, "breaking bulk is where the distributor buys in large quantities and then offers any amount of the product to customers. This is very important to the value-add functions provided by distributors because, as I mentioned earlier, many customers prefer to order only a small quantity at a time. Many manufacturers, like us, find it uneconomical to fill small orders and

Understanding the Value of the Middleman

will establish minimum order requirements to discourage them. By buying large quantities from manufacturers and breaking down these 'bulk' orders into smaller quantities, distributors provide customers with the ability to buy only the quantity they need. In fact, they generally pass the savings of buying in bulk on to the customer. So the price charged to the final consumer, the patient in our industry, pays less than if the hospital tried to order directly from us."

customers through a well-trained outside sales force. A distributor salesperson is considered an important asset by providing a wide range of advice such as inventory planning, advertising, office layout, customer service, and product applications. As I mentioned earlier, some medical equipment distributor salespeople provide technical product assistance for doctors in the operating room while they use the product in an operation. I couldn't afford to have you spending your days in operating rooms advising doctors; I need you

Adding Value

Manufacturers	Customers
Make sales contacts	Provide product availability
Hold inventory	Assortment convenience
Process orders	Customer service
Gather market information	Break bulk
Provide customer support	Advice and technical support

"So the distributor actually *lowers* the price for the final consumer? I thought that middlemen companies always increase costs. Interesting..." Thomas mumbled.

"Finally, distributors provide *advice and technical support* to focused on building new products for us to sell. And it's not just the technical products that require advice and technical support. Even nontechnical products may need a certain amount of technical advice and assistance for proper use."

Understanding the Value of the Middleman

"Wow, I didn't realize the value that distributors bring to the marketplace," offered Thomas.

"I know and you're not alone. Many people don't know what the industrial distribution industry is all about. It's not advertised on TV or Internet sites that most people visit, so I can see why you never heard of this industry. It's actually quite fascinating and quite large. About $3 trillion worth of products are sold through distributors every year in the U.S. People don't really get into the industry for the sexy products, but rather they get into it for the people. The people that work in this industry are very interesting and they like to have fun. My guess is that we'll have a good time at our visit."

"So, what are the alternatives to distributors? I mean, if we don't use this company are there other methods to sell our product in the marketplace?" asked Thomas.

"Well, there are manufacturers' representatives, or selling agents, we could use. They basically provide the selling coverage for manufacturers who can't do it themselves. These reps generally represent several non-competing manufacturers at the same time and typically work on 100% commission and don't take title to the product. Essentially, manufacturers' reps provide excellent market coverage, sales contacts, order processing, customer service and marketing information. I've looked into them, but would rather give the first shot for selling our product to a distributor."

"Another category," continued Bob, "is a broker. Similar to manufacturers reps, brokers operate on commissions, they don't take title to, or physical possession of, what they sell, and often not actually seeing the product. Brokers typically function as go-betweens by finding and locating buyers for products and identifying buyers for specialty or used items. Brokers tend to be deal makers and typically represent manufacturers in areas where the manufacturer has no other distribution source. Brokers are typically used for agricultural products, metals and refined petroleum products. I don't know if they will be useful for us. Our customers feel very comfortable buying from distributors, so I hope our conversation today goes well."

"From the sound of it, so do I," replied Thomas, "and thanks for helping me see the light about how we sell the products we make. I didn't realize how this market worked."

Understanding the Value of the Middleman

"Well, don't get too confident, there's lots more to learn about how industrial distributors operate. I'll be discussing a variety of strategic issues in our meeting that I haven't covered with you," responded Bob just as the plane started to land on the runway.

CREATING AND MANAGING SUCCESSFUL SUPPLIER RELATIONSHIPS

LEARNING OBJECTIVES

After studying this chapter, you should be able to:

- Explain why distributors need effective supplier partnerships and strategic alliances.
- Understand the important factors in developing successful partnerships.
- Evaluate supplier performance.

INTRODUCTION

"A company isn't a person. It's made up of persons. When you develop a business relationship, it's really the sum of those parts."
—Damon Jones, Chief Operating Officer, Miller Heiman.

Selecting the right suppliers and negotiating good financial terms with them are vital steps in ensuring distributor profitability. Distributors rely on thin margins, so developing strong, "win–win" relationships with partners is crucial for maintaining long-term competitive advantages. High performing distributors take a strategic approach to the manufacturer selection process. They know that strategic supplier relationships will create value for all participants—an insight reflected in the saying: "A distributor is only as good as its suppliers."

Effective supplier partnerships have a "mutual commitment over an extended time to work together to the mutual benefit of both parties, sharing relevant information and the risks and rewards of the relationship."[1] A high level of trust, low level of conflict, open exchange of information and clear expectation of future performance characterizes these relationships.[2] For example, Bristol-Myers Squibb (BMS) treats suppliers as an extension of BMS staff. By sharing knowledge of how BMS operates, the company promotes collaboration and continuous improvement, lowers risk, and enhances supplier services and support.[3] Unfortunately, not all supplier partnerships succeed; there are indications that 50 percent of all strategic alliances fail prematurely.[4] This failure is often the result of goal conflict between manufacturers and distributors. By understanding one another's business objectives, manufacturers and distributors can predict—and prevent—problems.

---

[1] Definition of supplier relationship from the Institute for Supply Management, (http://www.ism.ws/index.cfm).
[2] Kumar, N., Scheer, L.K., and Steenkamp, J.B.E.M. (1995), "The Effects of Supplier Fairness on Vulnerable Resellers," *Journal of Marketing Research,* 54 (February), 54-65.
[3] Supplier Relationship Management at Bristol-Myers Squibb, Caps Research, September 2003 (accessed July 1, 2014; https://knowledge.capsresearch.org).
[4] Dun & Bradstreet survey, 2000, (accessed June 25, 2014; http://www.dnb.com/supply-management.)

The Manufacturer's Goals

A manufacturer has three primary goals when working in the distribution channel:

- *Expand market reach*: Manufacturers use distributors to enhance their market reach and gain access to targeted market segments and individual customers.
- *Enhance brand value*: Manufacturers rely on the resources and capabilities of distributors to provide value-added services that enhance their brands and increase perceived customer value.
- *Minimize costs to serve*: Manufacturers rely on distributors to reduce the costs and investments associated with marketing their products to end-use customers.

Achieving these goals simultaneously is difficult; manufacturers may be required to make trade-offs. As we will see, these trade-offs often cause problems for distributors.

The Distributor's Goals

Distributors focus on the assortment of products and services sold to end-users. Most seek to represent a variety of quality brands in the marketplace. Unlike manufacturers, who focus on one product line, distributors view their businesses as one-stop shops where customers can choose from a variety of competing brands. Distributors base their business models on two main goals:

- *Maximize inventory turnover*: Distributors are current-asset–intensive businesses; they constantly strive to increase turnover of inventory and accounts receivable. In fact, distributors often use the phrase "inventory turnover equals cash." By increasing turnover—selling more products and collecting on debts—distributors enhance revenue figures on their income statements.
- *Maximize margins*: Distributors seek to increase the contribution margin (profitability) of each transaction. When the difference between the price the manufacturer charges and the price at which distributor sells the product is bigger, the distributor enjoys a greater margin.

A significant difference between manufacturers and distributors is that manufacturers seek to benefit from *economies of scale*, while distributors seek *economies of scope*. In other words, manufacturers aim to spread out their fixed costs by selling large volumes of a single product; distributors spread out their fixed costs by selling a large variety of products in a single transaction. Therefore, manufacturers and distributors will achieve goal congruence by balancing the manufacturers' goals of maximizing market access, optimizing brand value, and minimizing cost-to-serve with the distributors' goals of maximizing both turnover and margin.

One of the barriers to manufacturer–distributor goal congruence is that distributors represent competing product lines from multiple manufacturers. Each of those manufacturers expects the distributor to emphasize its product line over other brands. However, when a manufacturer's product line represents less than two percent of a distributor's business, there is less financial incentive for the distributor to maintain a close relationship with that manufacturer.[5] The distributor's dealings with the manufacturer become more distant and transactional. On the other side of the relationship, manufacturers also take into account the volume of business expected from a particular distributor (above or below the two percent threshold in sales or profits), but they ask additional questions such as: Can this distributor effectively handle promoting our brand over the competitive line? Is this distributor allocating the proper amount of salesperson "mindshare" to our brand, compared to competitive brands? Does multiple representation of competitive products compromise the market or financial objectives of our brand? The answers to these questions help manufacturers make strategic decisions about partnerships with distributors.

DEVELOPING SUCCESSFUL CHANNEL RELATIONSHIPS

True business partnerships are hard to create; failure rates are reported to be as high as 60 percent.[6] The most frequently cited reasons for partnership breakdown include (1) slow payback results, (2) poor communications, (3) over-optimism, (4)

---

[5] Narus, J. A. and Donath, B. (2009), *Build, Fix, or Terminate: The Distributor's Guide to More Profitable Supplier Relations,* NAW Institute for Distribution Excellence.
[6] Speckman, R.E., Isabella, L. A. and MacAvoy, T. C. (2000), *Alliance Competence: Maximizing the Value of Your Partnerships,* New York: John Wiley & Sons.

lack of shared benefits, (5) lack of commitment to relationships, (6) misunderstanding of operating principles, (7) cultural mismatches and (8) lack of effective relationship experience. Strong business-to-business relationships require commitment and hard work. We next discuss several important factors that contribute to successful B2B partnerships.

Trust

The notion of trust in B2B relationships is "the firm's belief that another company will perform actions that will result in positive outcomes for the firm as well as not take unexpected actions that result in negative outcomes."[7] In a manufacturer–distributor relationship, there is an implicit understanding that the success of each company depends on the other firm's efforts to satisfy the customer. Mutual trust enables the manufacturer and distributor to share information and jointly achieve results. Research suggests that trust empowers partners to take risks to maintain their relationships that include (1) making candid statements about motives and priorities, (2) making the first move toward a large concession that seeks reciprocation, (3) taking unilateral action to reduce tension and (4) making a proposal for compromise.[8] Although there are problems and conflicts in all business relationships, high levels of trust will motivate parties to probe for deeper understanding and search for constructive solutions. In essence, trust between a manufacturer and distributor is the foundation of a profitable relationship.

Personal Relationships

As noted previously, the manufacturer–distributor alliance is a relationship between individuals. Interpersonal relationships are important; proper alignment of people from both sides, at all levels, is critical for maintaining a successful relationship. When members of two companies are linked through common interests and degrees of decision-making authority (finance to finance, manufacturing vice

---

[7] Anderson, J.C. and Narus, J.A. (1990), "A Model of Distributor Firm and Manufacturer Firm Working Partnerships," *Journal of Marketing*, 54 (January), 42-58. See p. 45.
[8] Dwyer, R.F., Schurr, P.H. and Oh, S. (1987), "Developing Buyer-Seller Relationships," *Journal of Marketing*, 51, 11–27.

president to distributor vice president), the partnership stands a higher chance of achieving long-term success.

Shared Vision and Goals

While many manufacturer–distributor relationships fail because their goals are poorly aligned or overly optimistic, successful partnerships have realistic expectations about sales volumes, profits, and service related goals such as on-time delivery. It is neither feasible nor necessary to be explicit about every aspect of a business relationship, but it is important for partners to share an overall vision and agree on clear objectives. For example, a distributor with a good reputation for product availability and post-sales service would be a poor fit with a manufacturer that is slow to process stock orders, or non-supportive of post-sale service training.

Commitment

Manufacturers and distributors with successful relationships are committed to shared improvement and growth, starting at the highest levels of management. When top executives of both companies actively support the partnership, the relationships are more likely to thrive. Top managers have the authority to foster workplace cultures and attitudes that allow the relationships to flourish. When conflicts inevitably arise, management-driven relationships result in a more collaborative approach to resolution, compared with relationships that are more arm's-length or transactional in nature.

Information Sharing

A free flow of information through formal and informal lines of communication is another characteristic of successful manufacturer–distributor relationships. Distributor feedback on the manufacturer's performance is an example of formal communication. A non-scheduled discussion of customer needs between company representatives is an example of informal communication. In both cases we recommend establishing customized systems to share information and avoid conflict. Along with encouraging open communication, successful relationships also require confidentiality of sensitive financial, process and product information. For example, when manufacturers give distributors advance product information or training, they may require them to sign a nondisclosure agreement.

Culture of Managing Change

As Charles Darwin said: "It is not the strongest or the most intelligent who will survive but those who can best manage change." In business, change is constant. There are shifting trends in global sourcing and distribution, intense competitive pressures, rapid advancements in technology, increased customer sophistication, and a greater emphasis on supply chain effectiveness and efficiency. These changes are fueling a shift toward relationship-oriented buying. If partners are not equipped to manage the uncertainty associated with change, their relationship has a greater chance of failing. Managers coping with rapid change become distracted from their core businesses, resulting in a loss of focus on relationships. A study that examined the speed of supply chain firms' reactions to changes in the marketplace reports that almost half of the companies surveyed (45 percent) took one month or longer to respond to supply chain changes. Nearly one-quarter (22 percent) of respondents took three months or longer to respond to market-induced changes.[9] The lack of change management abilities within the supply chain may be a cause of the low success rate of supply chain partnerships. Successful businesses are able to react quickly, allowing them to stay focused on their core operations and strategic relationships.

Culture of Continuous Improvement

In addition to staying ahead of change, manufacturers and distributors need to practice *continuous improvement*, which is the process of making a series of small improvements over time that eliminates waste in a system. Manufacturers and distributors with successful relationships continuously improve their capabilities to meet customers' demands for low costs, quality products, and efficient, on-time delivery systems. They know that establishing joint processes to correct and prevent mistakes takes a lot of effort. Partners must agree on a set of performance measures that monitor and measure continuous improvement.

---

[9] "Agility, Business Intelligence, and Your Supply Chain," Grant Thorton (January 6, 2014), report access July 4, 2014 from: http://www.grantthornton.com/issues/library/articles/distribution/2014/01-supply-chain-ingenuity-survey.aspx#sthash.OFOYO8QI.dpuf

Talent-Based and Technology-Based Capabilities

Distributors seeking strong, sustainable relationships with manufacturers need to have two kinds of resources in place: *talent-based capabilities* and *technology-based capabilities*. Firms with talent-based capabilities manage relationships by assigning suitable staffing, in terms of both numbers and skill types, to the task. Research shows that one of the best practices of top-performing companies is the use of cross-functional teams to achieve common objectives.[10] These versatile teams are able to collaborate both internally and externally.

Companies with technology-based capabilities have the appropriate technological and logistical capabilities to meet cost, quality and delivery requirements. Less technologically advanced distributors struggle to maintain long-term relationships with manufacturers that have high technology and responsiveness expectations. Conversely, however, manufacturers should have the flexibility to respond quickly to distributor requests to meet changing customer needs. Before entering into any long-term partnership, manufacturers and distributors must conduct a thorough investigation of each other's technology and talent-based capabilities.

Performance Metrics

Distributors can improve their relationships with manufacturers by establishing a performance metric evaluation system. Measures used to assess manufacturer performance typically focus on delivery, flexibility, costs (products, transportation), and total cost of ownership. The goal of an evaluation system is to provide relevant, results-driven metrics that are easy to understand. Performance feedback provides both parties with a snapshot that identifies manufacturer strengths and weaknesses. Distributors often provide manufacturers with further feedback on inventory levels, turnover of the manufacturer's product, customer fill rates, order cycle time and customer satisfaction. Manufacturer evaluation systems improve communication between companies, reduce risk and provide data based scorecards that improve relationships. By using these methods, companies rely on quantitative assessments rather than emotions to assess performance.

---

[10] Hannon, D. "Best Practices: The Hackett Group Outlines the Best Practices

As we have seen, many factors need to be in place for manufacturer–distributor relationships to succeed. Even so, other forces can strain relationships. Increased transaction costs, fewer obstacles to switching to a different supplier, the dropping or minimizing of a brand, and changes to personnel can all result in diminished value of partnership. Sometimes, manufacturer–distributor relationships fail simply because competitors provide better deals in terms of pricing, product quality or warranties, and manufacturer rebates.

MANUFACTURER EVALUATION AND CERTIFICATION

As we noted previously, distributors must have a manufacturer evaluation process in place to identify their most reliable suppliers and target them as strategic partners. By developing partnerships with their best suppliers, distributors can leverage supply chain expertise, gain competitive advantages, and create new opportunities to develop value-added processes for their customers. The multi-attribute evaluation model provides distributors with a systematic way to rate the performance of their suppliers.

The Multi-Attribute Model for Evaluating Suppliers

Many companies use the multi-attribute evaluation model to evaluate and certify their suppliers. An example of the evaluation process, shown in Table 1, illustrates the following steps:

1. Select key dimensions of performance that are acceptable to both the distributor and the supplier.

2. Monitor and collect performance data.

3. Assign numerical weights (importance) to each of the dimensions. These should add up to 1.0.

4. Rate each performance dimension between 0 and 100, with 100 representing a perfect score.

5. Multiply dimension rating by weight, and sum the overall score.

6. Classify vendors based on their overall score:

- Unacceptable (less than 50): Supplier needs immediate corrective action or may be dropped from the product line.
- Conditional (50–70): Supplier needs additional work in some areas; may be a candidate for replacement, depending on future performance.
- Certified (70–90): Supplier meets performance standards.
- Preferred (90–100): Supplier exceeds performance standards.

7. Audit and perform ongoing certification review.

Table 1
Multi-Attribute Model for Evaluating Suppliers

Performance Measure	Importance of Performance Measure	Performance Rating	Weighted Performance Value
Product availability	.25	90	22.50
On-time delivery	.25	80	20.00
Percentage of delivery quantity correct/no shipping damage	.10	80	8.00
Communication of delays	.20	85	17.00
Responsiveness (e.g., handling rush orders)	.10	70	7.00
Business (e.g., information sharing, attitudes)	.10	80	8.00
Total score	1.00		82.50

Notes: With a total score of 82.50, this company would be classified as a Certified supplier, assuming 80.00 is the cut-off for certification, and 90.00 is the criterion for being classified as a Preferred supplier.

The list of performance measures shown in Table 1 is not exhaustive, but distributors should keep in mind that increasing the number of dimensions will increase the cost of evaluation. In our example, product availability and on-time delivery are the most heavily weighted performance criteria, making up 50 percent of the total evaluation. Distributors typically assign heavier weights to these two dimensions; they also place strong emphasis on the supplier's ability and willingness to communicate delays in delivery. Since delays are inevitable, delivery updates are highly valued by distributors.

The multi-attribute model is compensatory; a high performance in one dimension can compensate for a low performance in another (assuming the two are of equal or near equal in weight of importance). One drawback of using this evaluation model is that it is time consuming and costly to collect data on each supplier as rating each supplier on multiple dimensions (such the six used in our example) requires an in-depth analysis of each supplier's performance. Distributors with many suppliers may need to adjust the amount and quality of information they collect about each supplier. Nevertheless, the model clarifies performance expectations, and results in a healthier dialogue between companies as they work together to develop expectations for high performance.

The multi-attribute model for supplier evaluation is an internal method; there are other, less onerous ways to evaluate manufacturers. External certifications such as ISO 9000 and ISO 14000 are globally recognized indicators of companies that meet certain high quality standards.

ISO 9000

The International Organization for Standardization (ISO) developed ISO 9000 in 1987. The designation is a series of quality assurance standards for design, development, production, installation and service. Certification is a third-party determination of quality that is recognized around the world. Thus, U.S. distributors should expect prospective suppliers to have some type of ISO 9000 certification, especially when contemplating dealings with unfamiliar, international manufacturers. ISO 9000 certification provides assurance to the distributor that the manufacturer has met an internationally recognized level of quality. (Note that although we refer simply to ISO 9000, there are many categories and numerical versions of IS0 9000 quality standards.)

ISO 9000 is a unique certification. Companies that apply to become ISO 9000 certified must adhere to the following principles of quality:[11]

- *Principle 1—Customer Focus*: Organizations depend on their customers and therefore should understand current and future customer needs, meet customer requirements and strive to exceed customer expectations.
- *Principle 2—Leadership*: Leaders establish unity of purpose and direction of the organization. They should create and maintain the internal environment in which people can become fully involved in achieving the organization's objectives.
- *Principle 3—Involvement of People*: People at all levels are the essence of an organization, and their full involvement means their abilities can be used for the organization's benefit.
- *Principle 4—Process Approach*: A desired result is achieved more efficiently when activities and related resources are managed as a process.
- *Principle 5—Systems Approach to Management*: Identifying, understanding, and managing interrelated processes as a system contributes to the organization's effectiveness and efficiency in achieving its objectives.
- *Principle 6—Continual Improvement*: Continual improvement of the organization's overall performance should be a permanent objective of the organization.
- *Principle 7—Factual Approach to Decision Making*: Effective decisions are based on the analysis of data and information.
- *Principle 8—Mutually Beneficial Supplier Relationships*: An organization and its suppliers are interdependent and a mutually beneficial relationship enhances their ability to create value.

ISO 14000

The ISO developed ISO 14000 in 1996 as a series of international standards for environmental management. In 2004, the organization amended the standards to make them compliant with ISO 9000, making it possible for businesses to earn

---

[11] The eight quality management principles are from the ISO.org web page, accessed July 7, 2014 (http://www.iso.org/iso/qmp_2012.pdf).

combined certification of their environmental and quality management systems. (As with ISO 9000, there are several numerical versions of ISO 14000).

To achieve ISO 14000 certification, firms must produce cost savings by conserving materials and reducing water and energy use. These savings lead to reductions in other costs, including permits, worker compensation, insurance, legal fees, and fines. ISO 14000 firms benefit from an enhanced public image and decreased liability for waste cleanup costs. The certification process embeds sound environmental management in the culture of the firm. In the future, as more organizations achieve ISO 14000 certification, they are likely to pass on expectations and requirements to their suppliers, leading to demands for environmental sensitivity throughout the supply chain.

SUPPLIER RELATIONSHIP MANAGEMENT

Supplier relationship management (SRM) is a set of capabilities that enhances manufacturer–distributor collaboration, execution and performance monitoring. Supply chain businesses use SRM software to streamline processes and enhance communications between buyers and suppliers. The specific capabilities of SRM programs are vendor-dependent, but all SRM products share five key features:

- *Visibility*: Product flows and manufacturer–distributor information is more visible. Access is customizable by role and aggregated in a single portal.
- *Automation*: Automation of transactions between distributors and manufacturers frees up resources to allocate to other value-added areas.
- *Integration*: A multiple department view is available to internal and external users.
- *Collaboration*: The ability of a manufacturer to enter information directly into a distributor's system provides real time updates to inventory and products in transit.
- *Optimization*: Warehoused data can be accessed easily using dynamic optimization tools, which optimizes decision making.

Distributors that invest in SRM software are able to access a wealth of information about their businesses and their suppliers. They can answer the following questions:

- Are we focusing on the right set of manufacturers?
- What are the competitive rankings of our best suppliers?
- How are our suppliers performing with respect to costs and on-time delivery?
- How can we achieve greater buying efficiencies?
- Are there consistent supplier performances across various warehouses and facilities?

Although SRM implementation requires extensive employee training, it provides quick access to data and information and answers important strategic questions. Automating supplier activities can lead to significant cost savings and allow distributors to focus on value-added activities such as collaborative planning. Prior to SRM implementation, buyers typically spend 10 percent of their time on supplier relationship development, 40 percent on expediting purchases, and 50 percent on order processing and shipment tracking. Following SRM implementation, buyers spend 50 percent of their time on collaborative planning, 30 percent on supplier relationship development, 10 percent on expediting, and 10 percent on exception management. By implementing SRM, distributors can meet their strategic goals of increased inventory turnover and cost reduction.

SUMMARY

Distributors are constantly managing a variety of supplier relationships. These relationships vary from close, collaborative partnerships to arms-length, transactional affiliations. Key takeaways for this chapter include:

1. **Understanding the differences between manufacturer and distributor goals.** True strategic partnerships result when manufacturers and distributors align their goals and share resources and capabilities.
2. **Explain the factors underlying successful relationships.** Research has uncovered nine factors associated with strong manufacturer-distributor relationships; 1. Trust, 2. Personal relationships, 3. Shared vision and goals, 4.

Commitment, 5. Information sharing, 6. Culture of managing change, 7. Culture of continuous improvement, 8. Technology-based and talent-based capabilities, and 9. Performance metrics.

3. **Explain how to measure manufacturer performance.** The multi-attribute model of performance evaluation is a linear quantitative model for assessing supplier performance. However, managers from both sides should meet periodically to examine the outcomes of these assessments and make plans for improvement. ISO 9000 and ISO 14000 are two internationally adopted standards to indicate assurance of quality and environmentally friendly processes, respectively.

4. **Understand supplier relationship management.** Organizations that successfully implement supplier relationship management can improve decision-making processes and relationship quality, reduce costs and risks, and achieve higher performances.

DISTRIBUTOR DEMAND FORECASTING

LEARNING OBJECTIVES

After studying this chapter, you should be able to:

- Explain why demand forecasting in distribution is important.
- Identify key criteria used in market segmentation.
- Compare and contrast qualitative and quantitative forecasting techniques.
- Assess the accuracy of forecasts.
- Explain collaborative planning, forecasting, and replenishment (CPFR).

WHAT IS FORECASTING AND WHY IS IT IMPORTANT?

Successful, well-managed distributors know where their customers are located and how much and when they will buy. They are very good at forecasting future demand and revenues and are able to forecast a market comprised of many types of customers with varying needs. How do they do it?

High growth companies succeed by selecting well-defined groups of potentially profitable market segments and developing a distinct value proposition that meets or exceeds each segment's needs. In the business-to-business (B2B) distribution industry, this value usually is accomplished with a targeted mix of products and services. Successful firms also focus their marketing and selling efforts on acquiring and retaining profitable customers.[1]

The starting point in developing accurate sales forecasts is to understand how the company generates revenues within three broad B2B sectors: commercial businesses, institutions, and government. It also is important to segment each sector further, into smaller markets. By doing so, a company develops separate forecasts for each *market segment*, which is the term used to describe a group of customers with a common characteristic that predicts their response to a supplier's marketing stimuli.[2] Understanding various market segments is typically the first step in developing an effective go-to-market strategy. Forecasting experts focus on unique characteristics and segment needs to define the focus and direction of that strategy. Market segment research cites the crucial elements of the marketing mix that distributors need to not just satisfy but delight their customers. The added benefits of effective segmentation and forecasting for the distributor include lowered inventories, reduced stockouts, smoother fabrication and kitting plans, and reduced overall costs. More broadly, improved distributor forecasts benefit all trading partners in the supply chain, including manufacturers and end users.

At some point in their careers, all distribution and marketing managers will be asked to estimate the market potential and sales potential for their markets. This assignment can be tricky, because the number of users and the purchase

---

[1] Hippel, Eric von, Stefan Thomke, and Mary Sonnack (1999), "Creating Breakthroughs at 3M," *Harvard Business Review*, 77 (September-October), p. 47-57.
[2] Mitchell, Vincent-Wayne and Dominic F. Wilson, (1998), "Balancing Theory and Practices: A Reappraisal of Business-to-Business Segmentation," *Industrial Marketing Management*, 27 (September), p. 429-455.

rate change over time. A decline in prices, industry promotions, or changing economic conditions can also influence the size of the market. Not surprisingly, evaluating a market's potential is thus more of an art than a science. We define *market potential* as an estimate of the maximum demand over a period of time, based on the number of potential users and the purchase rate. Market potential for minivans, for example, could be characterized as the total number of households that have two or more children. Of course, actual sales would be less than market potential, due to a variety of factors, such as affordability and personal preference. The industry purchase rate therefore is a function of price levels, promotional expenditures, and the number of dealers selling minivans.

Company *sales potential* is much narrower than market or industry potential and is defined as the maximum portion of the total industry demand that a firm can sell within a period in optimal conditions. Company sales will always be lower than industry sales (unless the company is a monopoly). To understand a company's market share, you would need to calculate the ratio of company sales to industry sales.

Estimating Potential

All estimates of potential are based on two key components—the number of possible users of the product and the maximum expected purchase rate. Sometimes estimates of these numbers can be obtained from trade associations or commercial research associations, but often the figures must be self-generated and broken down by geographical area, industry, and customer type.

An efficient way to gain insight into the market potential for a particular industry is to use secondary sources. A wide variety of commercial data available for purchase provide information about the number of possible buyers, sizes of competing firms, ages of customers, income levels, and locations. Dun & Bradstreet and Equifax both sell commercial data for individual use. A free alternative source of business data is the U.S. government, which compiles comprehensive data on every business in the country. For example, the U.S. Census of Manufacturers is a report compiled every five years that combines North American Industry Classification System (NAICS) codes with other relevant aggregated business data. The NAICS (formerly known as the SIC code) sorts every business in the United States into sectors or groups that are assigned specific codes. Each code groups businesses that are similar in terms of the processes, raw materials, and parts used (if they are manufacturers).

The first step in using census data to estimate these potentials is to identify all the NAICS codes that make use of the product or service being investigated. This can be done by selecting industries that are likely customers, using expert judgment to choose appropriate codes from the NAICS manual, and running surveys of various types of firms to find where products are being employed. The next step is to select an appropriate database to support estimates of the amount of product used by each NAICS code.

A food machinery distributor in North Carolina, for example, could review past sales data to determine the relationship between the number of its machines in use and the number of production workers in a particular industry. As shown in Table 1, if the distributor found that 24 machines were used for every 1,000 grain milling employees, 15 for every 1,000 bakery workers, and 3 for every 1,000 beverage workers, it could determine the market potential for North Carolina. If the most recent Census of Manufacturers shows that North Carolina has 811 grain milling workers, and 24 machines are used per 1,000 workers, the market potential would be .811 x 24, or 19.5 machines. Similar calculations for other codes yield a total market potential of about 165 machines for the state of North Carolina. The accumulated potential for North Carolina, added to estimates derived for other states, then reveals the calculated national figures. These figures can be converted into annual measures of market potential by adjusting for the average life of the machines. If the machines last an average of 10 years, 10 percent of the North Carolina potential of 165 units, or 16 machines, would be replaced each year. Multiplying annual demand potential by the firm's current market share produces estimates of company potential.

Table I
Estimating the Market Potential for Food Machinery Distributors in North Carolina

NIACS Code	Industry	(1)* Production Employees	(2)** Number of Machines Used per 1000 Workers	Market Potential (1) x (2)
3112	Grain Milling	811	24	19.5
3122	Tobacco Mfg.	9,328	15	139.9
3121	Beverages	1,757	3	5.3
	Total Demand			164.7

*The production employee data could be gathered from the most recent Economic Census of Manufacturing (www.census.gov/econ/manufacturing.html), Geographic Area Series, North Carolina.
**Estimated by the distributor on the basis of past sales data.

Caution is warranted when using aggregated secondary data though, because the accuracy of a market potential estimate depends strongly on several factors, such as (1) the accuracy of the usage factor in representing underlying demand, (2) the quality of the data used, and (3) the extent of forecasting distortion caused by using averages, gross estimates, or proxies for products or services. Sometimes there is no reasonable way to estimate future values, due to the lack of meaningful historical aggregate data. If this were the case, then companies would need to employ qualitative forecasting methods, which are discussed next.

QUALITATIVE SALES FORECASTING

Qualitative methods of sales forecasting, also known as subjective techniques, use informed judgments by others together with various rating schemes. These techniques are popular when little numerical data are available to incorporate into a forecast. New products offer a classic example of limited information; qualitative methods frequently serve to predict sales revenues for these items. Qualitative methods also are recommended when managers or the sales force are particularly adept at predicting sales revenues. In addition, qualitative forecasting methods can be helpful in markets disrupted by strikes, wars, natural disasters, recessions, or inflation. In these conditions, historical data are not reliable, and judgmental procedures that account for factors causing market shocks are usually more accurate. Qualitative methods also can adjust mid- or long-range forecasts and quantitatively generated forecasts. Managers should calculate and record the forecasting errors produced by the qualitative techniques they employ, so that they know when to employ these methods. Most qualitative forecasts are based on executive judgments, sales force projections, surveys, and market tests.

There are at least two potential problems inherent to qualitative forecasting. First, bias can be introduced into the forecasts, because of the limitations on the forecasters' abilities to acquire and process complex information without being influenced by factors other than those pertinent to their decision. Second, qualitative forecasting is relatively expensive, because collecting the data takes managers and analysts a lot of time to complete. Despite these limitations, their use is widespread, and four of the most commonly used qualitative techniques are the jury of executive opinion, the Delphi method, sales force composites, and customer surveys.

Jury of Executive Opinion

The *jury of executive opinion* technique involves soliciting the judgment of a group of experienced managers to give sales estimates for proposed and current products. The main advantages of this method are that it is relatively fast and includes many subjective factors, such as competition, economic climate, weather, and other external factors that affect a company or product line. United Parcel Service forecasts come from a group of senior executives who use economic indicators, such as the Consumer Price Index, historical sales data, and other trends. These forecasts then get compared with predictions developed by salespeople, and the differences are reconciled. The continued popularity of the jury of executive opinion method shows that most managers prefer their own judgment to other, less well-known statistical forecasting procedures. However, available evidence suggests that, while an effective method overall, it does not lead to *more* accurate forecasting than other methods. Perhaps the main problem with this method is that it is based on experience, and it is difficult to teach someone how to forecast without having a nuanced understanding of the marketplace.

Delphi Method

The *Delphi method* solicits the input of experts, either internal or external to a company, and proceeds as follows:

1. Each member of the participating panel writes an answer to the question being investigated (e.g., a forecast of product or industry sales) and the reasoning behind this forecast.
2. The answers of all panel members are summarized and returned to the participants anonymously.
3. After reading the summary of replies, each panel member either maintains his or her forecast or reevaluates the initial forecast and submits a new one (and the reasons for changing it) in writing.

The answers get summarized and returned to panel members as many times as necessary to narrow the forecast range. This technique can be thought of as a "virtual" jury of executive opinion, because the executives do not meet face to face. The anonymity allows each member to use personal reasoning to develop a forecast, without the influence of strong personalities or the boss's pet forecast. It also reduces the effects of "groupthink" on the decision-making process. Because participants do not meet face to face, the influence of a strong leader or bias stemming from group members' desire to support one another is minimized.

Sales Force Composite

A favorite forecasting technique when intimate knowledge of customer plans is important is the *sales force composite method*. Using this procedure, salespeople project sales volumes for customers in their own territory, aggregate the estimates, and submit them to higher management levels for review. Many B2B distributors favor this technique because salespeople tend to be relatively accurate in their near-term or intermediate-term assessments of customers' needs. As a result, the sales force composite method is preferred when intimate knowledge of customer plans is important because close buyer–salesperson relationships are the best sources of information about customer purchasing plans and inventory levels. Research also suggests that salespeople are more active contributors to the sales forecasting process when they: (1) are properly trained to gather and incorporate key customer data into the forecast, (2) receive feedback about the accuracy of the measures and effectiveness of their forecasting efforts, and (3) understand their forecast's impact on resource allocations throughout the company.[3] When salespeople provide input, they buy into the forecast and are more likely to achieve their sales quotas. Most companies also integrate the sales force composite sales forecast with a more top-down approach though, to ensure the efficacy of sales force–generated forecasts.

Customer Survey

If a company has sufficient resources to undertake market research, it can conduct *customer surveys* to obtain inputs to its forecasting efforts. A company can use a variety of methods, such as face-to-face interviews, focus groups, telephone surveys, and e-mailed surveys to obtain information on anticipated purchases of new or existing products. The data generated by these surveys can provide information on anticipated product demand or anticipated economic activity; they assist in qualitative mid-range (monthly or quarterly) or long-range (one to five years) product or industry sales forecasts, as well as in qualitative adjustments to short-range product forecasts. When manufacturers survey their distributors (i.e., their customers) and/or distributors survey their customers in an attempt to understand future demand, the entire supply chain operates more smoothly. Customer data also can be used with sophisticated quantitative techniques to reveal meaningful insights.

QUANTITATIVE SALES FORECASTING

Our quantitative sales forecasting will focus on three time series approaches, moving average, weighted moving average and exponential smoothing. *Time series techniques* use historical data, ordered in time, to project trends and sales growth rates, with the assumption that past sales patterns apply to the future. However, before we begin our discussion of these forecasting methods, it is important to understand how seasonal factors influence future predictions. In monthly or quarterly sales forecasts, seasonal factors often are responsible for short-run fluctuations in sales data. Forecasts that appear accurate may become inaccurate due to a failure to consider seasonal factors. To improve accuracy, many firms make adjustments to eliminate seasonal effects.

---

[3] Byrne, Teresa M. McCarthy, Mark A. Moon, and John T. Mentzer (2011), "Motivating the Industrial Sales Force in the Sales Forecasting Process," *Industrial Marketing Management,* 40 (January), p. 128-138.

Distributor Demand Forecasting

The first step in seasonally adjusting a time series is to collect sales figures for the past several years. By averaging sales for months or quarters across the years, a seasonal index results. In Table 2, four years of quarterly sales are averaged to give a rough indication of seasonal effects. These quarterly averages are then divided by mean sales for all quarters, to reveal the seasonal index numbers. For example, dividing the average sales of 580.0 for Quarter 1 over the four years of sales data by the mean for all quarters, that is, 792.50 (12680/16 quarters), the seasonal index is 0.73 (580.0/792.50). Therefore, seasonal factors typically lower first-quarter sales by 27 percent. In Quarter 2, the seasonal index of 1.13 (900/792.50) suggests that seasonal factors typically increase sales by 13 percent.

With seasonal index numbers, developed for each time period, it is easy to adjust the set of sales data seasonally. Actual sales, such as those in Table 2, get divided by the appropriate index numbers to produce a set of deseasonalized data, which in turn inform sales forecasts. For example, the deseasonalized sales data for the four quarters of the first year in Table 2 would be 671 (490/0.73), 681 (770/1.13), 776 (900/1.16), and 814 (790/0.97) for Quarters 1, 2, 3, and 4, respectively. The resulting forecasts then should be multiplied by the seasonal index for the forecast period, to make them comparable with regular sales figures. Although performing the seasonal adjustment might seem to complicate the forecasting process, it is critically important for ensuring the reliability of forecasts of future sales.

Table 2
Calculating a Seasonal Index from Historical Sales Data

Quarter	Year				Four-Year Quarterly Average	Seasonal Index
	1	2	3	4		
1	490	570	530	730	580.0	0.73
2	770	980	850	1000	900.0	1.13
3	900	890	920	980	922.50	1.16
4	790	620	880	780	767.50	0.97

Notes: Four-year sales of 12680/16 = 792.50 average quarterly sales.
*Seasonal index is 580.0/792.50 = 0.73.

Moving Averages

The *moving average method* is simply the use of past sales from several recent periods to predict of sales in the next period. The formula for the moving average is:

$$F_t = \frac{S_{t-1} + S_{t-2} + \cdots + S_{t-n}}{n}$$

where:
F_t = Forecast for the prediction period.
S_{t-1} = Actual sales for a given time period t occurrence (e.g., t – 1 would be sales one period prior to the predicted period).
n = Number of periods in the moving average.

An important assumption of the moving average approach is that the future will be an average of past sales. For example, if sales in the last two periods went from 490 to 770, as shown in Table 1, a two-period moving average forecast would be 630 (1260/2), as illustrated in the following exhibit. When there is a strong trend in a time series, a moving average forecast without a trend adjustment lags. However, this lag can be an advantage if sales change direction (suddenly increase or decrease), because the averaging effect helps smooth out unexpected changes. To increase the model's smoothing effect even more, the number of periods used in the moving average formula could be increased (e.g., using three or four periods instead of two).

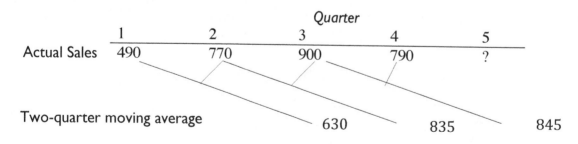

Forecasters next must decide how many periods (n) to include in the average. As the number of periods increases, the forecast reacts more slowly to changes in period-to-period sales fluctuations. That is, the forecast tends to smooth out fluctuations. Conversely, fewer periods in the formula respond more quickly to sales fluctuations. The optimal number of periods can be estimated by trial and error

Weighted Moving Average

The *weighted moving average* model is similar to the moving average model, with one exception: The moving average formula places an equal weight on each value being averaged, whereas the weighted moving average permits unequal weighting across prior time periods. In particular, the weighted moving average model allows forecasters to weight recent historical data more heavily than older data when determining the average. It is a suitable method when recent data are more representative of future demand than older data, and it allows the system to react more quickly to changes in sales. When weighting previous sales periods, the weighting factors are entered as percentages; typically, these percentages add up to 1.0.

The formula for the weighted average is:

$$F_t = W_1 A_{t-1} + W_2 A_{t-2} + W_3 A_{t-3} + \cdots + W_n A_{t-n}$$

$$\sum_{i=1}^{n} Wi = 1$$

where:
F_t = Forecast for the period being predicted.
W_t = Weight assigned to a time period t occurrence. Weights should add to 1.0.
A_t = Actual sales for a given time period t occurrence.

In applying this model to the preceding data, we would assume that sales for Quarter 3 (900) are due to some unexpected good fortune and do not reflect "normal" sales for the period. Using this model, we thus would weight Quarter 3's data lower than those from other quarters in the model. Because there are no prescribed weights, we need to "guestimate" the weights for each quarter. In predicting Quarter 5's sales using a three-quarter weighted average model, we might weight Quarter 3's sales as half as important as the other quarters. Thus, our model would use the following weights for each of the three preceding quarters: Q2 = .40, Q3 = .20, and Q4 = .40. Then predicted Quarter 5 sales would be 804 [(.4 x 770) + (.2 x 900) + (.4 x 790)].

Exponential Smoothing

Exponential smoothing is an alternative forecasting technique to the weighted moving average. A growing number of distributors and manufacturers prefer to use this technique because many forecasting software programs tend to incorporate an exponential smoothing function. It is also a fairly flexible model that can be used to either closely follow data trends or it can smooth out the forecast for unexplained data patterns. Essentially, the forecast for the next period's demand is the current period's forecast adjusted by some fraction (i.e., smoothing constant) of the difference between the current period's actual demand (e.g., current period sales) and the current period forecast. The smoothing constant is called alpha (α) which provides the relative weight assigned to the most recent demand. The exponential smoothing formula is:

$$F_{t+1} = \alpha(A_t) + (1 - \alpha)F_t$$

Where: F_{t+1} = forecast for the next time period.
α = smoothing constant, must be greater than 0 and less than 1.
A_t = actual demand for the most recent period.
F_t = forecast for the most recent period.

Another, perhaps easier equivalent formula to remember is:

$$F_{t+1} = F_t + \alpha(A_t - F_t)$$

While either of these formula can be used (the second formula is an algebraically equivalent version of the first), the logic underlying the smoothing constant α is that it is the relative weight assigned to the most recent demand. If $\alpha = 0$, then the forecast is equal to the last period's forecast (F_t) because no weight is given to the most recent demand. The value of α is typically between 0.1 and 0.6. The greater the α, the more responsive the forecast (F_{t+1}) is to demand changes, similar to the higher weight given to the most recent period in the weighted average model would make the forecast more responsive. The model's responsiveness to demand changes is illustrated with the following example.

Assume a small distributor had actual sales for a line of electrical components

Distributor Demand Forecasting

for the months of January through August (as shown in Table 3 below) and would like to forecast the demand for September using the exponential smoothing model. The first step is to start the model by using other forecasting method, such as jury of executive opinion, to estimate January's forecast. Actual sales in January were 269 and your firm estimated an initial January forecast of 280. These are the two data points needed to begin using the exponential smoothing model to predict the next period, in this case, February. You are also curious to to compare the model's predictions using two different α's of 0.3 and 0.6.

Using the exponential smoothing equation, the forecast for February would be 277 and 273 for α of 0.3 and 0.6, respectively and for March, the forecast would be 281 and 283 for α of 0.3 and 0.6, respectively. The remaining model predictions for April through August for the two alpha's are shown in Table 3 below. Note that September's forecast would be 272 for α of 0.3 and 271 for α of 0.6. Also notice how the 0.6 alpha forecast more immediately responds to the sales spikes in February and March than the 0.3 alpha forecast.

$\alpha = 0.3$	$\alpha = 0.6$
$F_{February} = 280 + 0.3(269 - 280)$	$F_{February} = 280 + 0.6(269 - 280)$
$F_{February} = 277$	$F_{February} = 273$
$F_{March} = 277 + 0.3(289 - 277)$	$F_{March} = 273 + 0.6(289 - 273)$
$F_{March} = 281$	$F_{March} = 283$
$F_{September} = 271 + 0.3(275 - 271)$	$F_{September} = 264 + 0.6(275 - 264)$
$F_{September} = 272$	$F_{September} = 271$

Table 3
Exponential Smoothing Forecast Example
A Comparison of α Alpha Weights

Month	Actual Sales	α = 0.3	α = 0.6
J	269	280	280
F	289	277	273
M	294	281	283
A	278	285	290
M	268	283	283
J	269	279	274
J	260	276	271
A	275	271	264
S		272	271

Estimating Forecasting Error

An important step in selecting an appropriate quantitative model is to determine the amount of error each model generates. It is important to estimate forecasts with historical data (actual sales data), using a variety of models, and to compare each forecast to actual sales to determine which model fits the data most closely. To compare forecasting accuracy across several time periods, many forecasting professionals use the *mean absolute percentage error (MAPE)*. These results appear in a percentage form that is easy to understand. The MAPE also can convey information when the item's demand volume is unknown. For example, telling the company president, "Our forecast was off by less than 3 percent" is more meaningful than saying, "We were off by 4,000 units." This benefit is particularly meaningful for distributors that deal with literally thousands of stockkeeping units (SKUs); it is very difficult to know a single SKU's typical demand volume.

Distributor Demand Forecasting

The formula for calculating the MAPE is:

$$MAPE = \left[\frac{\sum |Actual - Forecast|/Actual}{n} \right] \times 100$$

This method calculates the percentage forecasting error for each period, without regard to whether the errors are positive or negative, because it reveals the absolute value of the difference between actual sales and forecasted sales (for a particular period). The absolute value for each period is summed and the total is divided by the number of periods (i.e., obtain the mean). The averaged percentage forecasting error is then multiplied by 100 to arrive at the total percentage. The main advantage of the MAPE is that it allows for easy comparisons of forecasting errors across product categories and companies.

Table 4
Comparing Forecast Methods Using MAPE

Month	Actual Sales	Forecast Method 1	Forecast Method 2	$|e^1|$*	$|e^2|$	$|e^1|/A$	$|e^2|/A$
J	269	275	268	6	1	0.022	0.004
F	289	266	287	23	2	0.080	0.007
M	294	290	292	4	2	0.014	0.007
A	278	284	298	6	20	0.022	0.072
M	268	270	274	2	6	0.007	0.022
J	269	268	270	1	1	0.004	0.004
J	260	261	259	1	1	0.004	0.004
A	275	271	275	4	0	0.015	0.000
$\sum$(|Actual − Forecast| / Actual)						0.168	0.12
MAPE = (column sum / 8) × 100.						2.10%	1.50%

*$|e^1|$ = |Actual - Forecast|

Table 4 provides an illustration of using MAPE to compare two forecasting methods. The first step is to calculate the absolute difference between Method 1 and actual sales and the absolute difference between Method 2 and actual sales for each month, as indicated in columns $|e^1|$ and $|e^2|$, respectively. Then, each column gets divided by actual sales for the period (A). This is continued for each period in the model. Finally, the sum of each $|e^1|/A$ and $|e^2|/A$ column is divided by the number of periods used in the model and then multiplied by 100. This provides the final mean percentage of error for each forecasting model. The lower the forecasting percentage error, the better the forecasting model fits the data. Thus, the model with the lowest forecasting error should be chosen to predict future sales. In our example, the second forecasting method is preferable, because the MAPE of 1.50% is lower than the 2.10% MAPE from the first method.

Collaborative Planning, Forecasting, and Replenishment

Collaborative planning, forecasting, and replenishment (CPFR) is a forecasting approach that incorporates inputs from many functional areas within the company and forecasts from various partners in the supply chain. This information-intensive task typically requires assigning a staff member to gather, organize, and interpret the information. Imagine that a large regional electrical distributor is planning to implement CPFR and has put Kristen, an operations manager, in charge of the project. Kristen is responsible for organizing joint meetings within her own company, where marketing, logistics, sales, and procurement personnel discuss their plans for the forecasting period. By participating in these meetings, all parties that might influence the sales forecast also have direct input into the demand estimation process.

After compiling the inputs from the different departments and synthesizing each function's strategies and plans, Kristen reaches out to the company's customers and key manufacturers to assess their marketing, promotion, and sales plans for the products in question. She might gather this information through e-mail, telephone conversations, face-to-face meetings, industry conferences, and site visits for example.

After she gathers and synthesizes the external data, Kristen can share the resulting summary plan with the distributor's functional managers, then develop forecasted demand estimates. Finally, Kristen would develop a demand estimate for the forecast period, drawn from all the data available. With such comprehensive information sharing and input, including reliable forecasts from key customers and manufacturers, the CPFR approach generally results in very accurate forecasts.

DISTRIBUTOR OPERATIONS AND CHANNEL MANAGEMENT

LEARNING OBJECTIVES

After studying this chapter, you should be able to:

- Explain why distributors use the total cost approach to manage operations.
- Identify the key operational factors used in distributor operations.
- Explain the importance of managing inventory and the relationship of inventory to profitability.
- Explain the distributor metrics for determining service standards.

ADDRESSING A DRUG PROBLEM THROUGH BETTER MANAGED INVENTORY

Too little or too much inventory is the Achilles' heel of any distributor. Perhaps the most challenged industry from an inventory management perspective has been the health care industry. In particular, the management of drug inventories has, historically, been extremely inefficient; drugs are too often misplaced or stolen, and inaccurate forecasting of medication usage creates a tremendous amount of waste. Medical personnel constantly have to track down errant medication doses, which takes up valuable employee time. In response, some health-care facilities are turning to high-tech solutions such as radio frequency identification tags (RFID), password-protected dispensing machines, and roaming robots to deliver prescriptions. Even older pneumatic tube drug transport systems that quickly transport drugs around hospitals are being updated with new canisters that require specific types of badges and a PIN to unlock them at receiving stations.

However, at the University of Maryland Medical Center, the technology changes have been even more dramatic. The Center has started using mobile robots to deliver medications directly to nursing units. Pharmacy staffers can simply print a label, scan and place the medication in one of the robot's locked drawers, and enter a destination code into a software program that communicates wirelessly with the robot. The robot travels on its own to the designated unit, where a nurse uses a passcode and fingerprint scanner to retrieve the medication.

The introduction of robots to the Medical Center has vastly improved drug inventory management by minimizing defects, reducing costs, and maximizing patient safety. Delivery reliability (providing the right product) increased by 23 percent, and delivery predictability (providing it at the right time) rose by 50 percent. The per trip cost of robot delivery averages less than half the cost for hand delivery; in its first year of operation, robot drug delivery has freed up over 6,000 hours in personnel time.[1]

The University of Maryland case illustrates the use of technology to address inventory efficiency problems. However, there are countless other nontechnology examples of inventory gains achieved by better management that have saved companies millions of dollars. In this chapter, we address critical inventory management issues facing distributors, then broaden our discussion to include other

Distributor Operations and Channel Management

essential distributor operations and explore the customer-focused outputs that foster channel members' high performance.

A TOTAL COST APPROACH

A distributor attempts to achieve the desired level of customer service at the lowest cost by focusing on a *total cost approach*. Distributor managers pay special attention to the relationships between distributor functions involved in channel management, such as transportation, warehousing, inventory management, materials handling, order processing, and packaging. In the total cost approach, the separate costs of individual functions are measured by the extent to which an increase (or decrease) in one cost affects the other components and the overall costs. For example, using a faster, more responsive transportation carrier will likely increase transportation costs. But if the amount of inventory needed can be reduced, because the carrier provides a quicker resupply, so the warehouse and inventory carrying costs decrease. The inventory and warehouse savings may more than offset the higher transportation costs. From the standpoint of total distributor costs, the increase in costs for a faster carrier would be regarded as a good investment, because it would lower total distributor costs. The total cost approach to managing overall distributor operations is depicted in Figure 1.

Figure I

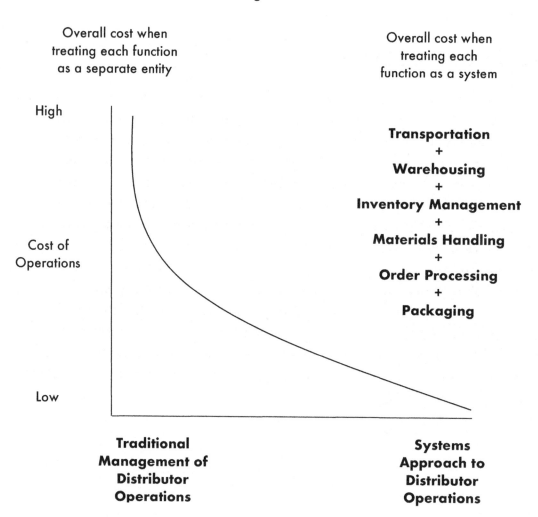

TRANSPORTATION

Transportation accounts for a high percentage of overall logistics costs—typically more than 60 percent of total logistics expenditures. Transportation managers are responsible for ensuring that inventory is available and properly positioned, in an economical manner. This responsibility is critically important to the overall functioning of the company, because poor performance in this operational aspect could irreparably damage customer relationships. As a result, successful firms have come to realize that order-to-performance cycles (e.g., "just-in-time" processes) reduce margins for error in transportation to near zero. It is beyond the scope of this book to discuss all aspects of transportation, but it is important to understand transportation fundamentals.

Transportation economics are a function of distance and weight. Distance affects transportation costs by contributing directly to fuel, labor, and maintenance. The tapering principle suggests that the cost curve increases at a decreasing rate as distance traveled increases. The weight principle indicates that the transport cost per unit of weight decreases as load size increases, because the fixed costs of delivery, pickup, and administration are spread over a greater distance. One implication of this principle is that, whenever possible, small loads should be consolidated into larger loads to maximize economies of scale. Other factors that affect the economics of transportation include product density (higher density products result in lower transportation cost per unit of weight), liability (improved packaging can reduce carrier liability), and market factors (whether the shipper returns "deadheaded" which means that the truck returns empty or finds a backhaul load to decrease costs).

To be effective and efficient in dealing with transportation issues, distributors must stay informed about the latest developments in logistics. The main challenge facing a distributor is choosing the optimum mode and routing of transportation to meet customer service demands, which can be a very complex task due to the number of issues that must be resolved. Some typical questions include:

- What are the costs and benefits of using owned carriers versus common (e.g., FedEx) carriers?
- What are the different rates and services offered by common carriers?
- How reliable are various common carriers?
- What transportation modes are competitors using?

When applying the total cost approach, a transportation manager trades off transportation cost increases (or decreases) with a calculation of how the potential changes will affect overall distributor operations costs. One way managers deal with these questions is by turning to technology-based solutions. For example, Rand McNally offers two software programs, MileMaker® and IntelliRoute®, designed to enhance efficiencies in transportation. According to Rand McNally's website[2]:

> MileMaker® provides industry standard Household Goods (HHG) and Practical routing that is used in millions of rating calculations every day;

while IntelliRoute® software helps fleets and shippers reduce costs and increase productivity by providing accurate, truck-specific mileages and routes. Rand McNally's industry standard software is used by 94% of the top motor carriers, the largest manufacturers and retailers in North America, 75% of IFTA agencies and is already integrated with over 82 transportation management applications.

The American Trucking Association reports that trucks move the vast majority (approximately 70 percent) of domestic freight tonnage.[3] The Association divides the industry into two major segments: less-than-truckload (LTL) and full-truckload (TL). An LTL freight shipment does not fill an entire truck; it is typically palletized, and its weight ranges from 150 lbs. to 10,000 lbs. Shipments over 10,000 lbs. are usually moved by a full truckload, but the shipping manner can vary according to factors associated with particular products.

Third-party transportation service providers (3PL) offer multiple options to carriers and shippers. They are usually generalists that expect to be compensated for providing an overall service, such as brokerage, freight forwarding, freight consolidating, warehousing, or information processing. Estimated U.S. spending on 3PL services for 2013 was $150 million, less than 10 percent of the approximately $1.6 trillion spent on logistics by all U.S. firms that year.[4]

Most people are familiar with 3PL companies such as United Parcel Service (UPS) and Federal Express (FedEx), but many other less known brokers and freight forwarders also provide logistical services. *Transportation brokers* function as intermediaries between shippers and carriers and typically do not take possession of the product. They use their networks and their access to a library of freight carriers to select the appropriate carrier for a particular need. *Freight forwarders* move cargo from one point to another and assume responsibility from the place of receipt (origin) to destination. Freight forwarders earn part of their profits from the difference between truckload and less-than-truckload shipping rates. Surface freight forwarders must register with departments of transportation and maintain minimum cargo insurance.

WAREHOUSING

A key distributor function is to hold and store products in facilities until they are sold—a simple concept that often requires answers to many, complex questions.

Five of the most frequent questions refer to (1) the location of warehouse facilities; (2) the number of warehouse units; (3) the size of the warehouse units; (4) the design of the units, including layout and internal systems; and (5) whether to own or rent the facility. Answering these questions requires careful planning and analyses, as well as potential input from local experts such as real estate brokers and industrial engineers. However, a few key principles inform all warehousing decisions.

Decisions about the location and number of warehouses should include the required customer service levels (measured by delivery service reliability and frequency), as well as the costs of developing, stocking, and operating multiple warehouse locations. These decisions often involve a trade-off between fewer warehouses (lower costs) and longer delivery frequencies. To choose the number of warehouses, it is also important to consider the geographic distance that can be serviced by a warehouse using typical transportation modes. For example, with trucks, a single warehouse can serve a market area of 200 miles within one travel day, 450 to 500 miles within two days, and 700 to 750 miles within three days (depending on weather and road conditions).

A popular warehouse configuration is a *hub-and-spoke distribution system*. In this system, a *distribution center (DC)* serves a regional market by consolidating large volumes of inventory and providing stock to smaller regional warehouses that service customers. The hub-and-spoke system reduces transportation costs; due to higher volumes, manufacturers can use large trailers for shipments to the DC, while smaller trailers can deliver to customers.

Firms also use the hub-and-spoke distribution system to determine the number of warehouses needed to service their customers. For example, Fastenal is a large distributor of maintenance, repair, and operating (MRO) products. It operates more than 2,600 local "stores" across the United States, Canada, and Mexico. Each store operates independently and has its own smaller warehouse to stock inventory for the needs of its local customers. To service this many facilities, the company has strategically placed its 14 DCs around the country and maintains more than 300 trailer trucks.[5]

INVENTORY MANAGEMENT

Accurately managing inventory is critical to distributor profitability. Although seemingly a straightforward task, firms struggle to determine an "accurate" level of inventory. In theory, the optimal level is the lowest level of inventory that will enable the supplier to meet customer demand. While a more comprehensive discussion of inventory management principles can be found in logistics textbooks, we focus our attention in this section to some of the more essential concepts needed to run a distribution center. First, however, we present in Table 1 some basic inventory terms that distribution-based operation managers should be familiar with.

**Table 1
Inventory Definitions**

Inventory Policy	Guidelines for what to purchase, when to take action, and how many to order.
Service Level	Management-specified performance targets.
Order fill	Percent of customer orders completely filled.
Case fill rate	Percentage of cases or units ordered that are shipped as requested. A 98% case fill rate indicates that, on average, 98 of 100 cases ordered are filled from available stock.
Line fill rate	Percentage of order lines filled completely.
Performance cycle	Time between the release of a purchase order by a buyer and the receipt of shipment.
Average Inventory	Typical amount of inventory held over time.
Order quantity	Amount ordered for replenishment.
Safety stock	Extra inventory used to protect against demand and performance cycle uncertainty.
Obsolete inventory	Out-of-date stock or stock that has not experienced recent demand.
Transit inventory	Amount of inventory typically in transit between facilities on order but not yet received.

Distributor Operations and Channel Management

Because distributors tend to make money by selling larger volumes on smaller profit margins, firms try to keep their *inventory carrying costs* low without sacrificing customer responsiveness. Inventory carrying costs include financing, insurance, and storage, as well as the costs of damaged, lost, and stolen goods; they typically amount to 25 percent of the value of the inventory per year. Although these added costs can erode profitability, failing to maintain the necessary inventory to meet customer demand on a regular and timely basis would cause a firm to go out of business very quickly.

How can distributors determine the amount of inventory needed? In an ideal world, a firm would keep its inventory at the lowest possible level and place orders for goods in large quantities, because placing fewer orders helps lower ordering costs. However, these two objectives (low inventory levels and large order quantities) tend to conflict: Average ordering costs tend to *decrease* in proportion to the size of the order, and average inventory carrying costs tend to *rise* in direct proportion to inventory levels. Faced with this conflict, inventory managers need to trade off between the two costs to find optimal levels. How would you make such a trade-off?

Figure 2
Example EOQ Curve

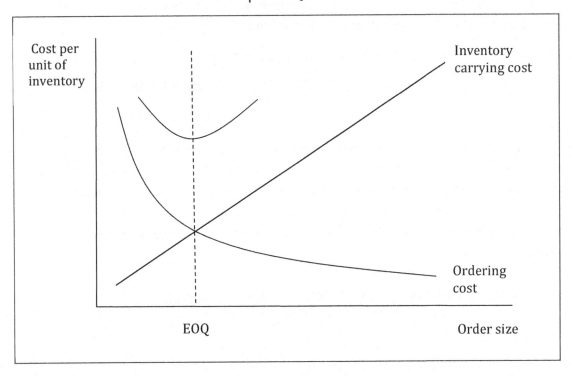

Economic Order Quantity (EOQ) Model

One way to find the optimal level of inventory is to use the *economic order quantity (EOQ)* formula. The EOQ occurs at the point at which total costs (in this case, inventory carrying costs plus ordering costs) are lowest. As shown in Figure 2, the distribution operations manager should attempt to achieve the lowest total cost by balancing inventory carrying costs and order costs.

To calculate the appropriate order quantity, a manager would use the EOQ formula:

$$\sqrt{\frac{2 \times Dy \times Cp}{Ch}}$$

where Dy = Demand for year.
 Cp = Cost to place a single order.
 Ch = Cost to hold one unit of inventory for a year.

Imagine that George is a distribution manager for a large electronics distributor. George forecasts that annual demand for an energy management switch is 16,000 units. The annual holding cost per unit is $2.50, and the cost to place an order is $50. What is the EOQ George should order?

$$\sqrt{\frac{2 \times 16000 \times 50}{\$2.50}} = 800 \text{ units per order}$$

By ordering the EOQ amount, a manager can increase inventory turnover by reducing the amount of time that inventory stays in the warehouse. *Inventory turnover* is the relationship between the cost of goods sold and the average inventory on hand, at cost. The old adage that inventory turnover equals cash coming in the door is just as appropriate today as it was years ago. A common inventory turnover calculation used in distribution is:

$$\text{Inventory turnover} = \frac{\text{Cost of goods sold during the period}}{\text{Average inventory on hand at cost}}$$

An inventory turnover of 4 means that the company replaces its inventory every quarter (or every 90 days). A faster inventory turnover means that a firm is using its inventory investment more efficiently. However, a high inventory turnover number also could imply that the firm (1) is not taking full advantage of quantity discount opportunities, (2) has lost sales due to frequent stockouts, or (3) uses poor sales forecasting and therefore must respond reactively by placing frequent inventory orders. When firms work to increase their inventory turnover, they significantly reduce inventory carrying costs—and sometimes can save millions of dollars.

A *just-in-time (JIT) inventory management system* aims to lower inventory costs. Proponents of the JIT system believe that excessive inventories are wasteful. The JIT inventory management system is complex, with several distinct characteristics that are worth noting. First, JIT systems tend to use only a few, nearby suppliers that receive more frequent, smaller lot deliveries than non-JIT delivery systems. Second, the JIT system relies on a "pull-oriented" demand schedule. In a pull system, inventories are not produced or delivered until they are requested. In a push system, production and delivery are initiated in anticipation of customer demand. Thus, the JIT system tends to need less *safety stock* (i.e., extra inventory used to protect against demand and performance cycle uncertainty). Third, most experts argue that the JIT system works best when a buyer's delivery schedule is smooth and predictable and suppliers are responsive to improvements, such as better labeling or container systems. For many distributors however, full implementation of a JIT system is not practical, due to their irregular customer demand.

Distributors often use an *ABC inventory analysis* to reduce their total inventory needs, such that they assign different customer service level requirements to their inventory on the basis of factors such as sales and profits. The ABC analysis further divides the inventory, so that the best-selling items ("A" inventory items) have the highest safety stocks. The 80/20 principle, which states that 80 percent of sales are derived from 20 percent of inventory items ("A" items), often gets applied. The "B" items typically represent 15 percent of dollar sales and approximately 30 percent of items, so they require lower levels of safety stocks than "A" items. The "C" items constitute only 5 percent of sales but 50 percent of all inventory items. As a result, they are ordered less frequently and may have only a target 80 percent in-stock service level, because of their low strategic priority.

MATERIALS HANDLING

Materials handling involves the range of labor activities and equipment used to place and move products in storage. An important issue when developing materials handling systems is finding ways to minimize the distances that products move within the warehouse while the distributor has possession of them (prior to sale). Decisions also seek to make the best use of labor when receiving, handling, and shipping products.

Renewal Windows, a division of Anderson Windows, provides a good illustration of how the company has changed its inventory handling processes. The company uses a highly automated system that can build an entire replacement window within 20 minutes, from design to shrink-wrapped product. The completed windows are lined up on the loading dock to be delivered to customers. Anderson's problem was that the windows were being placed according to production sequence, rather than the scheduled routes of the delivery trucks. The drivers and delivery personnel constantly had to rearrange the windows on the truck to find the next window to be delivered, which in turn led to a high number of broken windows. To fix the problem, Anderson altered its labeling in the finished inventory staging area, to be more consistent with daily transportation routes. This simple, but effective change saved the company thousands of dollars in inventory and manufacturing costs.

Another way firms lower their inventory handling costs is by *cross-docking*. When firms use cross-docking, the inbound inventory from an arriving truck moves immediately across the receiving dock and gets loaded onto trucks for dispatch to customers or warehouses. The inventory is never stored in the warehouse. This process minimizes handling and storing costs, because products move straight from receiving to shipping. The process also can be automated for the distributor, using sophisticated scanning technology and a smart system of conveyor belts. If the manufacturer includes the product's final destination in the bar code, a distributor can load the bar-scanned box onto a conveyor belt in the warehouse from the inbound truck. The box then passes through a scanner that reads its destination, and a smart conveyor belt system reroutes the box to the correct outbound truck waiting at the other end of the warehouse. No one touches the product, other than unloading it and loading it into the trucks. Cross-docking can reduce a distributor's per case handling costs by as much as two-thirds.

Distributor Operations and Channel Management

ORDER PROCESSING

One reason manufacturers rely on distributors to market their products is that distributors are able to fulfill customer orders. *Order cycle time* is an important metric for measuring order-processing efficiency; it is defined as the time between order placement and customer receipt. Inefficiencies in order processing due to cumbersome, wasteful processes slow down the order cycle time considerably. In response, some firms try to meet customer demands by using a faster mode of transportation, to make up for the slow order processing time, which increases the overall cost of customer service.

It may seem that fulfilling customer orders is easy, but it is actually very difficult to develop an efficient order processing system. Customers see only the result of a great deal of planning, training, and capital investment. Some larger distributors process many thousands of orders every day. Fastenal, the leading distributor of MRO products we described previously in this chapter, processes close to 30 million customer orders annually. To handle this vast array of orders accurately and efficiently, the company has developed a state-of-the-art automated order picking system that not only speeds up the order flow process but also helps it understand and forecast future regional product demands more accurately. The combination of Fastenal's order processing system and its more than 2,600 stores gives the company a unique competitive advantage in the marketplace. According to Fastenal, this quick and efficient order processing system is crucially important to its core mission of providing reliable product availability to its millions of North American customers.[6]

PACKAGING

Packaging is relevant to a distributor's operations because it affects overall costs and other components of the distribution system. For example, in an effort to cut transportation expenses, one manufacturer switched from wood to Styrofoam to crate its large transformers. Based on authors' personal conversations with the consultant who initiated the change, the company conducted a careful risk analysis which resulting in company executives concluding that it could save tens of thousands of dollars in shipping costs without increasing the risk of product damage.

In another case, 3M created a tube-shaped, reuseable mailing package, specifically designed to carry expensive computer chip wafers from companies such as Intel to high-tech fabricators that used the chips in their product. The tubes were designed to withstand almost any type of destructive force and could hold $100,000 worth of chips (approximately 10 wafers per tube). Prior to this innovation, chips were delivered one at a time to prevent damage. The new tubes, once emptied, could simply be dropped in the mail by customers, to be delivered back to the manufacturer for reuse. This uniquely designed package had widespread appeal in the market: It saved the industry thousands of dollars in shipping and handling charges.

These examples illustrate the point that packaging in the industrial market is far more than a promotional device for attracting customer attention. If designed properly, packaging not only enhances efficiencies in the channel of distribution but also provides a company with a competitive advantage in the marketplace.

DISTRIBUTOR METRICS FOR DETERMINING SERVICE STANDARDS

The main goals of distribution operations are to fulfill orders in a timely and efficient manner and to conduct other activities that maintain competitive advantages. Over the years, logisticians and other academics have formalized the types of services that can be measured as *service standards*. Before implementing any service standards though, distributors should determine precisely what their customers value in terms of service, because the higher the service standards required, the greater the costs. In a recent study of B2B industrial buyers, product availability and timely delivery were among the top five most important factors in supplier selection.[7] These results underscore the importance of maintaining adequate levels of inventory for key inventory items and offering a highly responsive transportation system with adequate backup procedures. The study also indicated that more than 60 percent of B2B buyers prefer suppliers that provide a means to purchase online. In a more general sense, these findings highlight the importance of segmenting customers on the basis of a systematic, research-oriented attempt to understand their service needs.

Customer research can also provide valuable information about channel member needs and problems in areas other than logistics. One study of more than 7,000 customers of an industrial distributor indicated that the inside sales force was significantly more important to its customers than the outside sales force. One customer summed it up by stating, "I like Joe [the outside salesperson] because Joe brings donuts every Friday." While the results were surprising to management, they provided excellent insight into future training programs for its outside sales force.[8] These findings suggest that the development of distributor service standards should not be based solely on the views of manufacturers or distributor managers; customer input is critical to understand the necessary service standards and levels of service.

Meeting and exceeding customer needs by getting the right amount of the right products to the right place at the right time is perhaps the most important strategic competitive advantage offered by the industrial distribution industry. This general statement of distributor value in the marketplace raises an important question: What are the measurable service performance indicators used to determine service quality? As noted previously, logistics researchers have developed various criteria of important service standards over the years. In one of the more frequently cited studies, Heskett, Galskowsky, and Ivie stress nine categories of logistics service standards:

1. Time from order receipt to order shipment.
2. Order size and assortment constraints.
3. Percentage of items out of stock.
4. Percentage of orders filled accurately.
5. Percentage of orders filled within a given number of days from receipt of the order.
6. Percentage of orders filled.
7. Percentage of customer orders that arrive in good condition.
8. Order cycle time (time from order placement to order delivery).
9. Ease and flexibility of order placement.[9]

Using these service standards, a firm would typically quantify the level of service desired and then measure actual performance against the standards. For example, the order cycle time standard—time from order placement to order delivery—might be set at 36 hours for 95 percent of all orders received. Therefore, for every 100 orders received, the firm must have 95 of the orders processed and delivered within 36 hours to meet the minimum standard. For the sixth category, percentage of orders filled, a firm might set the standard to fill 99 percent of customer orders. Then, only 1 of every 100 customer orders may go unfilled to meet that standard. Distributors operationalize their customer-focused performance by setting and meeting these types of standards. It is important to note that over time, channel members and customers' needs may change, and performance standards must be adjusted. Careful monitoring of the marketplace (competition, new products, customers) should help identify deficiencies before they become severe enough to inflict long-term damage on customer and manufacturer relationships.

---

[1] Laura Landro (2014), "Hospitals Address a Drug Problem: Software and Robots Help Secure and Monitor Medications," *Wall Street Journal*, (February 23, 2014) accessed May 12, 2014.

[2] From Rand McNally's web site http://www.randmcnally.com/product/milemaker, accessed May 14, 2014.

[3] *ATA American Trucking Trends 2014* report from the following web site: www.truckline.com/article.aspx?uid=d62a253d-b830-4fa3-b069-f7f8ff5d40df, accessed May 14, 2014.

[4] Global 3PL Market Size Estimates from Armstrong and Associates, http://www.3plogistics.com/3PLmarketGlobal.htm, accessed May 16, 2014.

[5] From the Fastenal website, https://www.fastenal.com/web/en/211/distribution-overview, accessed May 16, 2014.

[6] From discussions with Fastenal's Management Team and the company's web site (www.Fastenal.com), accessed May 20, 2014.

[7] UPS B2B Purchasing Insights, April 2014.

[8] Study conducted by the author for a large industrial steel distributor, May 2013.

[9] James L. Heskett, Nicholas A. Galskowsky and Robert M. Ivie (1973), *Business Logistics*, 2^{ond} Edition, New York: Ronald Press, 250-251.

ESSENTIALS OF DISTRIBUTOR PRICING AND PROFITABILITY

PART 1 Selling Price, COGS, Gross Margin and Mark-up

Terminology

List Price – advertised price. Rarely changed (annually), rarely charged (discounts)

Selling Price – list price minus trade and other discounts

COGS – cost of goods sold; the cost of merchandise to the distributor

Gross Margin – Selling Price minus COGS and adjustments (e.g. cash discounts taken)

Percent Gross Margin (PGM) – relationship between COGS and Selling Price expressed as a percentage.

Mark-up – difference between what distributor pays (COGS) and what the distributor sold it for (Selling Price)

Percent Mark-up (PMU) – mark-up expressed as a percentage.

Formulas

Gross Margin = Selling Price – COGS – Adjustments

PGM = (Selling Price) – (COGS) – (Adjustments)/Selling Price X 100

PMU = (Selling Price) – (COGS) – (Adjustments)/(COGS) – (Adjustments) X 100

Essentials of Distributor Pricing & Profitability

Gross Margin = Mark-up

PGM does not equal PMU

PART 2 Trade Discounts

Discounts are frequently given to distributors to reflect functions they perform and for bulk purchases. Additionally, they are often used to reflect changes in operating or raw material costs. Discounts allow for quick price changes without modifying list prices. Finally, multiple (chain) discounts are common.

Example: A copper wire manufacturer traditionally offers 25% trade discount to distributors. This month, the price of copper is down so the mfg offers an additional 10% discount. Finally, large orders receive an additional 5% discount. This discount would be referred to as 25, 10 and 5.

Formulas

Discount amount = (list price x discount percentage)

Selling price = list price − (list price x discount percentage)

Multiple Discounts (example above)

List price = $100 roll
Order Qty = 20 rolls

Invoice Price (LP x qty) = $2000

SP after 1st discount = $2000 − ($2000 x .25) = $1500
SP after 2nd discount = $1500 − ($1500 x .10) = $1350
SP after 3rd discount = $1350 − ($1350 x .05) = $1282.50

Essentials of Distributor Pricing & Profitability

Alternative Method – Multipliers

100 – discount percentage = multiplier

SP = LP x multiplier

SP after 1st discount = $2000 x .75 = $1500
SP after 2nd discount = $1500 x .90 = $1350
SP after 3rd discount = $1350 x .95 = $1282.50

To further simplify ---- chain multipliers together

$2000 x .75 x .90 x .95 = $1282.50

or

$2000 x (.75 x .90 x .95)
$2000 x (.64125) = $1282.50

How much was the discount?

List price – selling price = discount amount

$2000 - $1282.50 = $717.50

List price x (1 – multiplier) = discount amount

$2000 x .35875 = $717.50

Passing the Discount Along

Distributors often pass along some of the discount they receive to their customers.

Example: Copper wire manufacturer offers discounts of 25, 10 and 5; distributor offers discount of 15 and 10 to customer

$2000 x (.75 x .90 x .95) = $1282.50 (COGS to distributor)
$2000 x (.85 x .90) = $1530 (Selling price to customer)

Gross Margin = $1530 - $1282.50 = $247.50
PGM = $247.50/$1530 = 16%

What if the customer asks for an additional 5%?

Selling Price = $2000 x (.85 x .90 x .95) = $1453.50
Gross Margin = $1453.50 – 1282.50 = $171
PGM = $171/$1453.50 = 11.7%

Impact on Gross Margin to distributor:

Old GM – New GM/Old GM

$247.50 – $171/$247.50 = 31%

Giving an additional 5% discount to the customer reduces Gross Margin by 31%!

Cash Discounts

Not given as in the case of trade discounts. Cash discounts are offered and either taken or refused. To take the discount, the customer must pay early. Otherwise, cash discounts are treated just like trade discounts.

Essentials of Distributor Pricing & Profitability

PART 3 Finding PMU and PGM

Often a distributor would like to know the percentage gross margin associated with given percentage mark-ups

Example: Distributor typically marks up pumps by 25%. What percentage gross margin will be earned on such sales?

Selling Price = COGS × (1 +PMU)
$100 = $80 × 1.25

PGM = PMU/(1 + PMU)
20% = .25/(1.25)

Interpretation: Marking up a product 25% will return a 20% gross margin

Additionally, a distributor may have a target percentage gross margin to maintain and has to decide how much to mark-up a product to achieve the target PGM

PMU = PGM/(1 − PGM)
25% = .20/.80

Interpretation: To earn a 20% gross margin, the product must be marked up by 25%

ETHICAL DECISION MAKING AND THE DISTRIBUTOR

LEARNING OBJECTIVES

After studying this chapter, you should be able to:

- Explain why business ethics are important in B2B distribution.
- Understand how to make decisions that involve ethical problems.
- Recognize the common issues of distributor sales ethics.
- Understand how to build an ethics program.

WHY ETHICS ARE IMPORTANT

Ethics provide a moral framework to guide people in their business decision making. Specifically, *business ethics* refer to organizational principles, values, and norms that guide individual and group behavior. We continue to see an increased emphasis on ethics with companies instituting more rigorous ethical policies and training programs, and business schools devoting entire courses to the topic. This is due, in part, to the number of high-profile ethical scandals that continue to make headlines. Although many of these scandals result from unethical, often illegal actions by top executives, in many other examples, the unwise actions of just one salesperson have brought a corporation to its knees.

Ethical dilemmas are particularly prevalent in B2B selling because salespeople often must make decisions immediately while in the field in response to customers' demands and competitive offers. How a salesperson deals with these dilemmas reflects not only the person's character but also the company's culture and leadership. A distribution manager's decisions and actions often reveal and shape the moral character of his or her sales team. And sometimes these managerial decisions raise difficult and deeply personal questions: Do I have a different set of values at work compared with at home? How many of my values do I have to sacrifice to get ahead? Am I a different person at work? Answers to questions such as these are often matters of right versus right, not right versus wrong.[1] In other words, a manager must choose between two ways of resolving a difficult issue, where each alternative could be regarded as the right thing to do, yet it is impossible to do both.

Take, for example, a situation in which Bill Davis, district sales manager of an electrical distribution company, finds himself. Joyce, one of Bill's branch managers, wants to fire Mindy, a salesperson Bill hired last year, because she has been underperforming lately. Joyce, a single woman in her late twenties, was recently promoted to manager because of her success as a salesperson. She typically works longer hours than most other managers and has a serious, down-to-business personality. Joyce wants to fire Mindy because she believes Mindy has not fully developed her territory. Mindy is a devoted mother with full custody of her 5-year-old daughter and no child support or other assistance from her ex-husband. Joyce believes that Mindy's responsibilities at home have been keeping her from fully

---

[1] This section is based on: Joseph L. Badaracco, Jr., *Defining Moments: When Managers Must Choose Between Right and Right* (Boston: Harvard Business School Press), 1997.

realizing the territory's revenue potential for the branch. Because most other salespeople for the company are unmarried and in their early twenties, the long hours had not raised work–family issues previously.

On the one hand, Bill could allow Joyce to fire Mindy, because everyone else is working longer hours with no letup in sight, and she appears unlikely to be able to handle the continued competitive pressures the company still faces. On the other hand, Bill has serious reservations about firing Mindy. Company executives have said they want to create a "family-friendly" organization, and Bill has an opportunity to do something tangible to support this culture. Moreover, Bill believes that it is simply wrong to fire someone, especially a single parent, who is working diligently at her job.

Bill's dilemma illustrates our notion that managers' decisions often are not choices between right and wrong but between right and right. For a manager who struggles with these types of decisions, the stakes are very high. In this case, Bill's decision will reveal his basic values and provide a strong signal to other employees. In this sense, Bill's decision constitutes a potential "defining moment" in his management career.

Similarly, salespeople may face "defining moments" when the lure of an easy commission tests their ethical resolve. Literally hundreds of examples exist in which bad ethical decisions by salespeople have resulted in significant penalties for their company. Pilot Flying J, the nation's largest truck-stop chain, recently accepted responsibility for its salespeople who were skimming fuel rebates it owed its trucking customers and agreed to pay $92 million in penalties in a settlement with the federal government.[2] In another case, Johnson & Johnson agreed to pay $2.2 billion to settle U.S. Department of Justice allegations that the company's salespeople used deceptive sales practices to push its antipsychotic drug Risperdal. In this case, salespeople allegedly promoted the drug to doctors for unapproved, sometimes harmful uses.[3]

These two recent cases highlight the notion that an unethical salesperson's actions may result in serious legal problems for firms, but salespeople remain strongly influenced by their company's ethical climate. A morally ethical climate

---

[2] Betsy Morris and Cameron McWhirter, "Truck Stop Chain Reaches Settlement with Government," *Wall Street Journal,* (July 14, 2014), accessed www.wsj.com on July 15, 2014.
[3] Jonathan D. Rockoff, "Johnson & Johnson to Pay $2.2 Billion to Settle U.S. Probes," *Wall Street Journal,* (November 4, 2013).

enhances customers' experience by improving salesperson interactions and reducing salesperson turnover, due to their enhanced commitment to the organization. Other studies suggest that a positive ethical climate can increase trust in the sales manager, ethical selling behaviors, and job satisfaction—all of which are important elements for keeping the best salespeople from leaving.

A consistent theme across all of these studies is the competitive advantage gained by creating and maintaining a climate marked by high ethical standards. Because branch managers typically are responsible for establishing their business unit's ethical climate, they are critically important in training sales reps to recognize and respond appropriately to such situations. This chapter focuses on the ethical problems faced by distribution managers and B2B salespeople; it also provides a set of guidelines to improve one's ethical decision-making skills.

MODELING ETHICAL BEHAVIOR

Figure 1 illustrates a general model for making ethical decisions, including the factors that influence ethical decision making. Note that ethical values and standards derive not only from the workplace but also from family and religious backgrounds, the community and professional context, and the legal system. The figure demonstrates that business decisions represent a synthesis of the moral and ethical principles embraced by various entities. Conflict is common, because the values of the firm, as interpreted by its executives, may not match those of individual employees. Managers face difficult choices: Should they adhere to their own moral standards, rely on company policy, or act expediently to maximize short-run profits?

Some studies show that executives frequently choose expedient rather than moral solutions to ethical problems. For example, in one ethics survey, almost 50 percent of the 316 sales managers who participated reported they had heard their salespeople lie about promised delivery times to secure a deal.[4] The tendency of employees to abandon personal ethical standards in pursuit of corporate glory indicates that organizations need to foster a climate that reinforces ethical behavior. They must establish ombudsmen to provide salespeople with guidance on resolving ethical dilemmas; they might begin by developing a checklist that includes the essential steps in making ethical decisions.

---

[4] Eric Strout, "To Tell the Truth," *Sales & Marketing Management* (July 2002), pp. 40–47.

Figure 1
Making Decisions on Ethical Problems

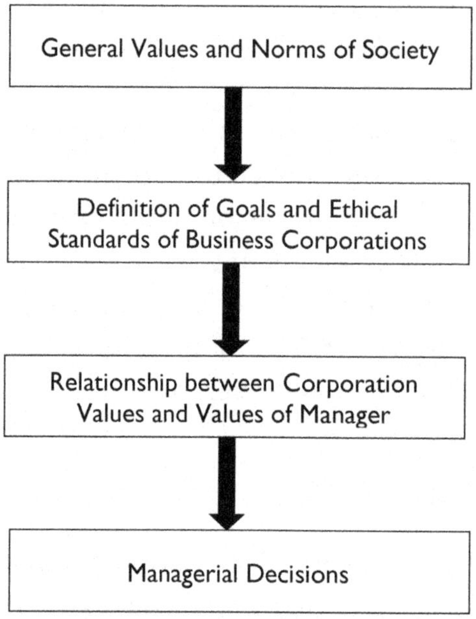

```
General Values and Norms of Society
          ↓
Definition of Goals and Ethical
Standards of Business Corporations
          ↓
Relationship between Corporation
Values and Values of Manager
          ↓
Managerial Decisions
```

Ethical Checklist

Managers need practical guidelines to help them confront ethical dilemmas and make difficult moral decisions. Some companies suggest using a simple checklist, such as the following, used by managers at General Dynamics:

1. Recognize the dilemma.
2. Get the facts.
3. List your options.
   - Are they legal?
   - Are they right?
   - Are they beneficial?
4. Make your decision.

By applying this checklist to our earlier example of sales manager Bill Davis's ethical dilemma, we explain how the decision-making process works.

Recognizing the Dilemma The first step in resolving any ethical dilemma is to recognize there *is* one. This may seem obvious, but research shows that employees' attitudes about their company's moral culture significantly affect their ability to identify ethical dilemmas in the workplace.[5] In our example, Bill recognizes that he faces the difficult decision of whether to fire Mindy, a salesperson whose results, though adequate, fall short of those achieved by other salespeople in Joyce's unit. Bill is correct in his assessment that his decision will have long-term consequences for the firm. He cannot make the decision lightly.

Assembling the Facts The next step in the ethical decision-making process is to assemble all the relevant facts. Although Bill should avoid micro-managing Joyce, he could get a better understanding of the situation by investigating Mindy's territory, customer base, competitors, and overall territory potential. He also could review aspects of Mindy's sales history, such as her revenues and gross margins, to make a more informed decision.

Making an Ethical Decision In most situations, there are no laws or court decisions to guide employees, so actions must be taken in the "twilight zone" between the clearly right and the clearly wrong. In Bill's case, he can use several approaches to address the issue with Joyce.

Shareholder vs. Stakeholder View. If Bill allows Joyce to replace Mindy, he will be making a personal commitment to a particular set of values. By establishing that the same high level of effort is expected from all sales staff, regardless of personal circumstances, Bill would be aligning his moral compass with the *shareholder view*. His decision would support the interests of the company's shareholders, customers, and owners, by assuring the highest profits possible. If however Bill does not allow Joyce to fire Mindy, he would be accepting the *stakeholder view* and choosing to protect employee welfare at the risk of reducing company profits. That decision would send a very different signal to the other salespeople about the basic values of the company.

At first glance, applying the shareholder view appears to be the most practical decision. However, this approach may not help Bill resolve all the issues. Replacing Mindy with an employee who has the same sales skills, but works longer hours, is likely to increase profits. But how much of that gain will be lost by the new

---

[5] "Ethics and Risk Management," *Global Association of Risk Professionals*, (June 21, 2012).

costs of recruitment and training, as well as the severance pay owed to Mindy? Stopping the grumbling of other salespeople about Mindy's underperformance may improve morale and productivity, but by how much? And how costly will the continuation of the company's high-intensity, "churn and burn" personnel practices be in the long run? Moreover, what are the costs of limiting the future talent pool by discouraging talented people from seeking jobs with the company? As we see, invoking the grand principle of maximizing profits adds little to resolving the practical issues Bill faces as he tries to make his decision.

Role Morality. The moral philosophies of sales managers are important for maintaining an ethical sales force, because managers are the ethics teachers of their organizations. They select field sales staff, provide ethical training, and enforce the moral codes of the firm. Both their actions and their omissions send moral signals. In describing individual moral philosophies, scholars have labeled two patterns of moral reasoning: *relativism* and *idealism*. A *relativistic manager* tends to reject universal moral rules and make decisions that are based on personal values and the ramifications of each situation. Idealists accept moral codes and believe that positive outcomes can be achieved by moral action. In general, *idealism* leads to better ethical decisions than relativism, with its elastic, "it all depends" approach. When 602 marketers answered a series of questions designed to measure relativism and idealism, the scores of sales managers were not significantly higher on relativism or lower on idealism than scores of other marketing personnel. This finding challenges the popular myth that sales personnel have lower ethical standards than those in other business occupations. The study also showed that relativism declines with age, idealism increases with age, and the idealism scores of women are significantly higher. When sales managers evaluated unethical sales scenarios, idealistic managers were more sensitive to the moral problems exhibited.[6] These findings suggest that basic moral philosophies such as relativism and idealism may have some influence on how a particular manager builds and maintains an ethical sales force.

Machiavellianism. Niccolò Machiavelli, secretary of state in the Florentine Republic in the sixteenth century, is known for his observations on human behavior and the workings of power. Many regard him as a realist—someone who focused on

---

[6] Ken Bass, Tim Barnett, and Gene Brown, "The Moral Philosophy of Sales Managers and Its Influence on Ethical Decision Making," *Journal of Personal Selling & Sales Management*, 18 (Spring 1998), pp. 1–17.

what is, rather than what ought to be. Machiavelli's political doctrine rejected the relevancy of morality in public life and regarded expediency as the guiding principle. He was prepared to manipulate people and bend the laws of business to achieve his own goals. The opportunism that characterized Machiavelli's philosophy is reflected in the following quotation:

> Any person who decides in every situation to act as a good man is bound to be destroyed in the company of so many men who are not good. Wherefore, if a Prince desires to stay in power, he must learn how to be not as good as the occasion requires.[7]

Applying *Machiavellianism* to Bill's workplace dilemma would lead him in a completely different direction. Machiavelli's advice to Bill would focus on how he could advance his own career with his decision about Mindy, or, at the very least, prevent Joyce from reducing his power by going over his head to higher executives. In this situation, Machiavelli's question to Bill would be, "Are you playing to win?"

Although dictionaries associate Machiavellianism with the principles and methods of craftiness, duplicity, and deceit, Machiavelli would have advised using such practices only for self-preservation. Unfortunately, some sales executives still use Machiavellian techniques to achieve personal or corporate goals. One survey of salespeople revealed that those with Machiavellian tendencies were less ethical than other salespeople.[8] The results suggest that sales managers should think twice about hiring people with Machiavellian inclinations and should teach their salespeople that those tendencies could influence ethical decisions in the field.

Conventional Morality. Another ethical standard that can guide the actions of executives is *conventional morality*, also known as *situation ethics*. This philosophy is reflected in the familiar phrase, "When in Rome, do as the Romans do." In this approach, the emphasis shifts from the individual to society; morality becomes what is acceptable to others at a particular time and place, and social approval is the ultimate test of right and wrong. With conventional morality, relationships with others are more important than results.

The conventional morality approach has no absolute ethical standards to guide the actions of executives. Morality is based on social convention and group consensus. If Bill used this philosophy to guide his decision about Mindy, the decision

---

[7] Niccolò Machiavelli, The Prince (New York: Mentor Classics, 1952).

Ethical Decision Making and the Distributor 80

would be based on consensus within the company. Bill's personal reluctance to fire Mindy would not determine his decision. As we can see, the problem with this approach is that the majority opinion might conflict with personal moral standards (in Bill's case) or even company policy. Sales staff sometimes justify cheating on expense accounts with the arguments that "everybody does it" or "it's a way to reward salespeople with tax-free dollars," even though these are not acceptable reasons for violating organizational policy.

Another problem with conventional morality is that it makes it difficult for managers to adapt to changing contexts or cultures. Ten dollars given to a headwaiter is a tip, but $10 given to a customs official to get a perishable product moving is a bribe. Although both transactions represent payment for extra services rendered, one is socially acceptable and the other is not—in the United States at least. What is moral, ethical, or common in one country is often unacceptable—or even illegal—in another. The hiring of relatives, for example, is regarded as nepotism in the United States; in South America, it is viewed as an honorable family duty.

COMMON DISTRIBUTOR ETHICS ISSUES

Sales managers must make decisions in a wide variety of situations that have ethical dimensions. These include colleague, customer, competitor, and other issues such as sexual harassment. As we discussed previously, there are no well-defined guidelines for moral conduct in these situations; the right course of action often depends on the circumstances. Our objectives are to raise some questions about business ethics and to identify potential problem areas.

Hiring and Firing

Various federal and state laws prohibit discrimination in hiring practices. Firms that hire only white male Christians between the ages of 25 and 30 years are clearly breaking the law. An ethical problem, in contrast, requires considerable judgment of the proper course of action—for example, whether to hire candidates who are relatives of officers of the firm.

Imagine that a sales manager must choose between a man and a woman for a field representative position. The woman is the daughter of a company vice president. Both candidates are well trained, but the man has somewhat more experience. If the hiring decision is based strictly on qualifications, the man should get the position. However, the firm is under pressure from the federal government to hire women. Should the woman be selected even though she has less experience? The sales manager knows there could be personal advantages in hiring the vice president's daughter, but choosing her could be regarded as reverse discrimination and be deemed unethical. With all of these factors in mind, the sales manager must make a moral choice between the welfare of the firm and personal advancement.

Another sticky ethical question is whether to hire salespeople from competitors. The main advantages of this hiring strategy are that the employees are already trained and likely to bring customers with them. Recruiting staff from competitors, however, can increase selling costs and lead to lawsuits if trade secrets are involved. Despite these risks, raiding competitors to fill positions is common across the B2B industry. Firms operate on the premise that it is easier to hire successful salespeople than it is to train them. To prevent such practices, some local competitors have unwritten agreements that they will not hire one another's salespeople. Although this arrangement helps to control selling costs, it often prevents salespeople from improving their positions by moving to other firms in the local area.

With so many firms concerned about reducing selling costs to boost profits, some companies are tempted to fire older salespeople who are paid high wages, to replace them with younger people who earn less. This approach is clearly illegal if it is part of a general plan to discriminate against older employees. The courts have ruled, however, that it is legal to fire older employees if the decision is based solely on the need to reduce costs.

House Accounts

A touchy problem for managers is how to handle large and important customers. These larger accounts often require special attention that exceeds the resources of the salesperson assigned to the territory. Should these accounts be left with the district salesperson or shifted to headquarters as "house accounts"? This is not an easy decision, because the accounts often generate high commission income. The designation of a customer as a house account is usually defended on grounds that it results in better service. However, the district salesperson who developed the account is likely to feel a proprietary interest because of the historical relationship with the client; a transfer to house account status is sure to be viewed as unfair by the salesperson losing the account. House accounts are one area where firms need a specific and well-communicated policy to avoid misunderstanding and resentment.

Expense Accounts

Most ethical abuse in a sales organization takes place with expense accounts. Salespeople are expected to spend money to contact customers, then get reimbursed for their expenses. Those who abuse the reimbursement policy often claim higher expenditures than the amounts spent. They keep the difference and do not report it to the Internal Revenue Service (IRS). In fact, one survey revealed that 25 percent of sales managers have caught a sales rep falsifying expenses within the past year.[8] Some would suggest that if all salespeople who pad their expense accounts were fired, there would be few left. Thus, managers must decide how tight the company's controls on expense accounts should be. Tight control on expense accounts could result in salespeople not traveling to contact out-of-the-way customers. However, generous repayment for expenses can invite IRS investigations and result in selling expense ratios that are higher than they should be.

A good solution to this problem is to monitor the actual expenses of some reliable salespeople for a month each year, then use these figures to set reimbursement amounts for all field reps. This approach greatly reduces the costs of processing expense accounts and keeps expense payments in line with actual experiences.

Gifts to Buyers

American business has a tradition of giving small gifts to buyers to express appreciation for past and future business. These gifts include novelties and samples given by salespeople or gift-wrapped bottles of liquor at Christmas. The problem is that the gift giving may start out with a pair of hockey tickets and end up as a portable television set for the customer's den. How can a gift be distinguished from a bribe?

A survey of sales executives revealed that 64 percent of those surveyed believed

---

[8] Ken Bass, Tim Barnett, and Gene Brown, "The Moral Philosophy of Sales Managers and Its Influence on Ethical Decision Making," *Journal of Personal Selling & Sales Management*, 18 (Spring 1998), pp. 1–17.

that a bribe was any personal gift to a buyer that exceeded a value of $100.[9] In the same survey however, 89 percent of the sales executives had witnessed colleagues offer potential clients personal gifts valued at more than $100. One way to differentiate a gift from a bribe is to determine whether the item is unexpected (a gift) rather than part of an agreed-upon payment for business (a bribe).

Today, purchasing managers appear more willing to accept gifts of clothing, pens, and calendars. However, management guidance on gifts has diminished, so it is increasingly difficult for salespeople to know what is right or wrong in a changing business environment. Some firms have set rules that prohibit buyers from accepting any gifts, meals, or favors that might compromise their integrity. Another guideline is the IRS ruling that only $25 can be deducted each year for company business gifts to any one individual. Although rules appear to solve the problem, they are hard to enforce. In the absence of explicit policies, sales managers and salespeople must apply their own judgment of whether an item is a gift or a bribe.

Bribes

As we have seen, the use of bribes to obtain business is widespread, so it is important to know what to do when it appears necessary to engage in this practice. Bribery is easy to spot in its most blatant forms. If a customer says it will place its order only after a $20,000 commission goes to a third party, the salesperson can be sure that someone is being paid off. Bribes of this size are unethical and likely illegal.

The president and top marketing executive of United Gunite Corporation both pleaded guilty in federal court to offering bribes to city officials throughout New Jersey for contract work worth millions of dollars. According to the executives, city officials expected "gifts" in exchange for their influence in getting lucrative contracts. These gifts ranged from furniture to designer suits to trips to Rio to, in one instance, a custom-designed waterfall for a backyard pool.[10] In another case, the vice president of sales for National Medical Care Inc. pleaded guilty to charges that he induced dialysis centers to order laboratory tests that were paid for by Medicare. In return,

---

[9] Melinda Ligos, "Are Your Reps Bribing Customers," *Sales & Marketing Management* (March 2002), pp. 33–40.

[10] Melinda Ligos, "Are Your Reps Bribing Customers," *Sales & Marketing Management* (March 2002), pp. 33–40.

the centers received rebates on certain products, consultant fees, and study grants.[11]

Foreign payoffs are so common that the U.S. Congress passed the *Foreign Corrupt Practices Act* in 1977, making it a criminal offense to offer a payment to a foreign government official to obtain or retain foreign business. However, other industrialized nations have been slow to follow. France, Italy, Belgium, and the Netherlands have yet to pass laws prohibiting either bribery or the deduction of bribes as a business expense for tax purposes.

Because of the competitive disadvantage caused by the Foreign Corrupt Practices Act for bidding on overseas contracts, the law has been amended; now U.S. companies break the law only if they knowingly make illegal payments. "Grease payments" are permitted, to facilitate a routine matter such as getting a visa or a permit, and it is now proper to make payments allowed under the written laws of a foreign country. Although these changes have improved competitiveness, U.S. firms still cannot engage in activities that local competitors in foreign nations carry out every day.

Unfortunately, much of the bribery and extortion in business dealings is disguised, making it even more difficult for the businessperson to choose right from wrong. For example, bribes have been disguised as gifts to hospital building funds, scholarships for relatives, memorial contributions, discounts on auto purchases, trips to professional meetings, golf outings, expensive dinners with speakers linking medical conditions to the utility of the sponsor's drug, research grants, and illustrated reference manuals.

Entertainment

Providing entertainment for potential customers is standard practice in American business, but it can lead to ethical problems. The issue is often "How much is too much?" Most would agree that taking a customer to lunch is fair, reasonable, and expected. Few would argue against occasionally taking a client and spouse to dinner and a nightclub. But what about the use of a company car or a weekend excursion on the company yacht? When big orders are at stake, it is common practice to fly personnel from the customer's plant to the supplier's headquarters for plant tours and introductions to corporate executives. Should the

---

[11] "Former Sales Executive at National Medical Admits Kickback Role," *The Wall Street Journal* (December 4, 1998), p. A15.

company cover the expenses of spouses taken on such trips? Is it ethical to offer customers free use of the company hunting lodge in Canada? Sometimes out-of-town buyers are provided access to prostitutes, in addition to other forms of entertainment. What legitimately and ethically constitutes "business entertainment"?

Sexual Harassment

The Equal Employment Opportunity Commission defines *sexual harassment* as follows:

> Unwelcome sexual advances, requests for sexual favors, and other verbal or physical conduct of a sexual nature constitute sexual harassment when (1) submission to such conduct is made either explicitly or implicitly a term or condition of an individual's employment; (2) submission to, or rejection of, such conduct by an individual is used as the basis for employment decisions affecting such individual; or (3) such conduct has the purpose or effect of substantially interfering with an individual's work performance or creating an intimidating, hostile or offensive working environment.

Workplace sexual harassment is prohibited by Title VII of the 1964 *Civil Rights Act*. Salespeople still encounter it though, even decades after it was deemed illegal and even as courts award more stringent violation penalties. In fact, salespeople are particularly vulnerable to "third-party harassment," which is harassment by someone outside the boundaries of the firm, such as a customer, vendor, or service person. An unfortunately typical situation arises when a male buyer from a key account asks a female salesperson for sexual favors in exchange for an order. In this case, the salesperson may need the order to help make her quota or fear the contract will be given to a competitor if she refuses. She may believe that if she complains, her boss will see her as lacking the selling skills needed to resolve the harassment problem. She may also worry that efforts to reform the buyer could sour relations between the two firms.

Many employees also are unaware that their own firm could be held liable for third-party harassment, which is prohibited behavior. All firms should develop formal policies for dealing with harassment that occurs inside and outside the organization. They should provide a process for salespeople to remove themselves from a harassing situation perpetrated by an outsider, without sanctions. Third-party harassers can be deterred by writing them a letter or by asking them to stop. These actions attract attention because they imply that the victim may take further, more public action. Some firms take a more passive response and simply reassign accounts with harassing buyers to new salespeople. Although this approach does not stop harassment, it may help the company retain the account.

Whistleblowing

A whistleblower is an employee who informs the public about an employer's or supervisor's immoral or illegal behavior. *Whistleblowing* is a last-resort action that is justified when the employee has the appropriate moral motive. There are several criteria to meet before making the decision to blow the whistle. First, the person who has observed the unethical behavior should have exhausted all the internal channels for dissent, including talking to a supervisor or the company ombudsman if one is available. Second, the whistleblower must be sure that the evidence is strong enough to convince the average person that a violation is taking place. Third, the observed moral violation should be serious enough to require immediate attention. Fourth, the act of telling the public should have some chance for success. From a practical standpoint, it makes no sense to complain to the public unless something is going to be done about the problem. Why expose yourself to hardship if there is no moral gain?

Whistleblowing is not taken lightly by employees, because they know they may suffer if they "go public" with a moral problem. A typical example of what happens to a whistleblower occurred when a West Virginia bank manager was fired for complaining that certain classes of customers were being overcharged. The manager sued the bank and won an unfair firing judgment, but he received only $18,000 after paying his legal fees. Worse, he was unable to find another bank job, even after applying to all the other banks in the state. He was eventually forced to take a lesser job as a state bank examiner.

Why are whistleblowers treated so badly for simply following high personal moral standards? The problem seems to be that by speaking out, they violate the *role morality* that demands that employees be loyal by keeping their mouths shut. Whistleblowing can embarrass managers, who often try to get rid of people they feel cannot be trusted. To encourage whistleblowers to come forward, federal laws have been modified to pay rewards of 15 to 25 percent of any recovery, plus attorneys' fees. As a result, in recent cases, whistleblowers have received an average reward of

$1 million. In one case, a company whistleblower won $77 million for alerting federal prosecutors to a scheme that bribed doctors to prescribe the company's drugs.[12]

Whistleblowing is caught in the classic conflict between the high ethical standards of individuals and the lower standards of morality often found in the business world. The optimal situation may occur when more firms set up formal internal mechanisms to ensure that employees who report moral problems are not ignored or punished.

GOVERNMENT REGULATION

When business fails to operate in an ethical manner, there is usually a public outcry for more *government regulation*. One of the basic roles of government is to set and enforce minimum standards of business morality. The judicial branch of government settles disputes over the interpretation of the regulations, and Congress writes new rules as they are needed. Some of the first government regulations in the United States related to business were designed to protect the public from noncompetitive activities. The Archer-Daniels-Midland Company, for example, was fined for scheming with four Asian competitors to rig the worldwide market for lysine, a livestock feed additive. ADM paid a $100 million antitrust fine, and two executives were each fined $350,000 for price fixing and sentenced to two years in prison.[19]

Consumer Protection

Federal laws also seek to set ethical standards for transactions between manufacturers and the consumer. For example, a common practice by which auto dealers inflated the prices of new cars ended when the Automobile Information Disclosure Act required manufacturers to attach labels to car windows showing the suggested price for the car, accessories, and transportation. Deceptive packaging has been targeted by the *Fair Packaging and Labeling Act,* which calls for standard package sizes and disclosure of the manufacturers or distributor's name. Attempts by loan companies and retailers to mislead consumers about interest rates led to the enactment of the *Consumer Credit Protection Act.* Truth-in-lending laws require full

---

[12] Charles Haddad and Amy Barrett, "A Whistle-Blower Rocks an Industry," *Business Week* (June 24, 2002), pp.126–130.

disclosure of annual interest rates and other charges on loans and credit sales. Recently, the *Magnuson-Moss Warranty Act* increased the power of the Federal Trade Commission (FTC) to regulate product warranties. New FTC rules require full disclosure of warranty terms and reduce the use of warranties as promotional gimmicks.

Why Are Regulations Needed?

Government often gets involved in business ethics when the problem is too big for individual firms to handle. For example, automobile exhaust is a major cause of air pollution, but it is difficult for an individual firm to solve the problem. If one company believes it is morally correct to install air pollution equipment in their cars, its costs will be higher than its competitor's costs. The ethically lazy firm's cars will be cheaper and more powerful, and they will literally run off with the market. In this situation, government regulation allows the well-intentioned business to be the good citizen it wants to be.

Many arguments exist for minimizing government's regulation of business. Businesspeople generally dislike government controls because they rob them of the flexibility needed to respond to changing conditions. Government rules established to solve problems in one decade are often obsolete by the next decade. For example, the federal government became involved in the regulation of natural gas prices because gas is often shipped through interstate pipelines. As might be expected, government entities tended to set low gas prices for maximum political gain. The drilling companies, acting more rationally, therefore slowed their search for new gas. As a result, the supply of natural gas declined until price controls were removed.

We believe there should be a balance between too little government and too much regulation, as occurred in the natural gas industry, where business was strangled by endless rules and red tape.

BUILDING A SALES ETHICS PROGRAM

Code of Ethics

The moral climate of a business reflects the words and actions of its top executives. If management tolerates unethical behavior in the sales force, there is little a member of the organization can do. Superiors set the moral climate and provide the constraints for making business decisions. The best way for a manager to build a strong sales ethics program is to get the backing of the board chairperson and the president of the company (Table 1). When this support is not available, there are certain to be ethical violations.

Table 1
Eight Ways to Keep Your Sales Force Honest

1. Get support from top management showing that they expect you to follow the spirit and letter of the law.
2. Develop and distribute a sales ethics policy.
3. Establish the proper moral climate. If the bosses follow the rules, then the troops are apt to do likewise.
4. Assign realistic sales goals. People who try to meet an unfair quota are more likely to rationalize their way to a kickback scheme.
5. Set up controls when needed. Watch people who live beyond their income.
6. Suggest that salespeople call for help when they face unethical demands.
7. Get together with your competition if payoffs are an industry problem.
8. Blow the whistle if necessary.

Once a sales manager gains the support of top management, the next step is to prepare a written *ethics policy statement* that informs the sales force that the company believes in playing fair with customers and competitors. Research shows that salespeople in organizations with *codes of ethics* perceived their work environments to have more positive ethical values, compared with salespeople who lacked ethical guidance.[13] A survey of 218 salespeople indicated that field reps welcome written policies that help them perform their jobs ethically.[14] The policies need to be monitored on a regular basis to ensure they are germane to the current selling arena. The advantage of a written ethics policy is that it allows a firm to be

---

[13] Sean Valentine and Tim Barnett, "Ethics Codes and Sales Professionals' Perceptions of Their Organizations' Ethical Values." *Journal of Business Ethics* (October 2002), pp. 191–200.

[14] Alan J. Dubinsky, Marvin A. Jolson, Ronald E. Michaels, Masaaki Kotabe, and Chae Un Lim, "Ethical Perceptions of Field Sales Personnel: An Empirical Assessment," *Journal of Sales & Marketing Management* (Fall 1992), p. 18.

explicit about which activities are permissible and which ones violate company standards, which can be especially useful when a customer, supplier, or boss asks an employee to participate in a shady deal. If the company has a code of ethics, the reply can be, "I'm sorry, but company policy forbids that," graciously ending the conversation. The vast majority of firms involved in foreign payoff scandals had no written policies regarding commercial bribery. Today, most firms claim to have formal ethics codes, but only half ask employees to acknowledge or sign them.[15] This finding suggests that some firms need to make sales reps more aware of their companies' ethical standards.

An excellent example of a written code of ethics comes by General Motors, which outlines its policy in a 12-page document, complete with instructional scenarios featuring fictional characters.[23] In one scenario, a purchasing employee visits the home office of a potential supplier, who offers him a ticket to a Rams football game and a chance to mingle with top executives. In another scenario, an investment banking firm involved in a GM acquisition invites several GM employees to New York for a dinner and gifts of mantel clocks. In both these cases, the policy clearly states that the gifts should be refused. However, GM's policy provides some wiggle room for employees outside the United States. Workers in certain countries may accept meals, gifts, or outings to comply with local business practices and avoid a competitive disadvantage. Furthermore, GM employees can continue to provide limited gifts and meals to their customers, but the most expensive restaurant in town is no longer appropriate. Finally, GM's policy requires GM employees to avoid violating their customer's gift policy.

Sales managers must be prepared to enforce company policies related to bribery. They should take note of employees who appear to live beyond their income and set reasonable sales goals so that salespeople will not be tempted to cheat to reach an unfair quota. Salespeople should know they can ask for assistance when they encounter unethical situations. Finally, if payoffs become too widespread, the sales manager should meet with competitors to work out a set of standards for the industry.

---

[15] *The Wall Street Journal* (May 14, 1996), p. A1.

Ethics Training

This discussion has shown that field salespeople are involved in a variety of competitive situations that may tempt them to engage in unethical behavior. However, only 44 percent of firms include ethics as a topic in their sales management training programs.[16] This finding suggests that more attention to ethics training is needed to help salespeople function in today's business environment.

Managers should be aware that simply publishing a sales ethics code does not guarantee field sales representatives will follow it. Companies should offer classes to make sure employees know what to do in morally ambiguous situations. At one training session, a salesperson asked, "When I check in at a motel, I get a coupon for a free drink; can I use it?" The correct answer was that it would be acceptable to use the coupon, but it would be wrong to accept $50 to stay there in the first place. In the case of pharmaceutical salespeople, research has shown that sales reps should stress the importance of long-term relationships with doctors and develop training classes that enhance product and customer knowledge. Reps with the greatest expertise tend to act more ethically in their relationships with doctors.[17]

In addition, younger sales managers tend to be less idealistic and more relativistic in their ethical decision making.[18] These findings suggest the importance of adjusting training program content to meet the needs of various age groups. New hires and younger managers, for example, should receive material that emphasizes the importance of company ethical norms and values and offers examples of specific behaviors to avoid. For example, Honeywell recently replaced its vague employee policy manual with a detailed handbook. Some of the unacceptable practices spelled out in the handbook included catcalls and sexual jokes.

In addition to general sales ethics training, many companies provide training to prevent sexual harassment and find solutions to simulated moral dilemmas. By working through multiple scenarios, salespeople learn how to recognize problems, assemble facts, consider alternatives, and make decisions. For example, what should

---

[16] Rolph Anderson, Rajiv Mehta, and James Strong, "An Empirical Investigation of Sales Management Training Programs for Sales Managers," *Journal of Personal Selling & Sales Management*, 17 (Summer 1997).

[17] Rosemary R. Lagace, Robert Dahlstrom, and Jule B. Gassenheimer, "The Relevance of Ethical Salesperson Behavior on Relationship Quality: The Pharmaceutical Industry," *Journal of Personal Selling & Sales Management* (Fall 1991), p. 44.

[18] Bass, Barnett, and Brown, *The Moral Philosophy of Sales Managers and Its Influence on Ethical Decision Making*, p. 11.

a saleswoman do when a male customer makes a pass and puts his hand on her knee? The advice is that she should firmly remove his hand and say, "Let's pretend this didn't happen." Men are also offered advice on how to avoid crude jokes and other forms of intimidation when dealing with female buyers. The idea behind ethics and sexual harassment training is to make sure employees are equipped to handle the real-world issues they are likely to encounter when calling on customers.

SUMMARY

Sales ethics provide a moral framework to guide salespeople in their daily contacts with customers. Ethical dilemmas are common in selling, because salespeople often have to make decisions in the field in response to customers' demands and competitive offers. This chapter has equipped you with the following skills:

1. **Explain the moral bases for business ethics.** Sales ethics form a code of moral conduct that guides sales managers and salespeople in their everyday activities. Ethical decisions can be based on various moral rules, including stakeholder and shareholder views, idealism, relativism, the self-interest of Machiavellianism, or conventional morality.

2. **Understand how to make decisions that involve ethical problems.** Managers who score high on idealism tend to make the most ethical decisions. Perhaps the best way to solve ethical problems is the pragmatic approach, which involves an objective analysis of relevant facts and leads to rational decisions.

3. **Recognize the issues of common sales ethics.** Areas in which sales managers are likely to confront difficult ethical situations involve hiring, house accounts, whistleblowing, expense accounts, requests for payoffs, and customer gifts and entertainment.

4. **Discuss how to build a sales ethics program.** Building a good company sales ethics program includes the following: getting support from top management, developing and distributing a sales ethics policy, establishing a proper moral climate, assigning realistic sales goals, setting up controls when needed, suggesting that salespeople call for help when faced with unethical demands, and blowing the whistle when necessary.

ACCOUNT RELATIONSHIP MANAGEMENT IN THE CHANNEL OF DISTRIBUTION

LEARNING OBJECTIVES

After studying this chapter, you should be able to:

- Understand the steps in the professional purchasing process.
- Identify the various influences in the buying center.
- Explain the evolution of business relationships.
- Understand the factors necessary for a fully developed relationship.

INTRODUCTION

Mayer Electric Supply, headquartered in Birmingham, Alabama, is one of the nation's largest distributors of electrical supplies. According to the company's president, Wes Smith, a "culture of service and servant leadership" is key to its success. Smith believes that making the effort to develop this culture has given the company a competitive advantage in establishing long-term, collaborative relationships. However, the process of developing business-to-business (B2B) relationships can be difficult and time consuming. According to Charles Collat, Chairman Emeritus of Mayer Electric, "Establishing a partnership has emotional costs. You need to develop a very trusting customer relationship and need mutual reasons to lock into each other for a period of time." Collat adds that partnerships "require relationships with all departments. You need to effectively work with plant, marketing, logistics, and operations personnel—and in virtually every aspect of the business."

Mayer Electric put its culture to the test with its bid to become the preferred electrical supplier to ThyssenKrupp Steel's steel mill plant in Mobile, Alabama. The plant, with an area of 50 acres and a roof more than 15 times larger than the lid of the Superdome, has a huge demand for electrical supplies. Mayer Electric's executive team recognized the business opportunity but also understood the amount of work needed to demonstrate the company's value proposition and win the bid. To prove the company's commitment to ThyssenKrupp, Mayer Electric developed a customized book with detailed descriptions of its quality processes, data processing capabilities, company history, and company culture. Mayer Electric's management team traveled to Germany to meet with ThyssenKrupp's executives to present the Mayer story and demonstrate the commitment of the entire organization to the partnership. As a result, the team flew home with the contract.

This chapter focuses on building lasting and profitable relationships with customers, referred to as *accounts*. In professional selling, there are many different activities and transactions that take place within the context of an ongoing relationship. The Mayer Electric example illustrates some of the most important features of B2B marketing: teamwork, close cooperation between buyers and sellers, involvement of executives in strategic accounts, establishment of long-term relationships, value creation, and expectations of high levels of trust.

Salespeople or sales teams can manage account relationships by being aware of four key aspects of B2B relationships: (1) the purchase process, (2) the buying center, (3) relationship building, and (4) relationship binders. Although these concepts are relevant to all customer relationship strategies, there are variations in their relative importance and execution. For instance, expectations of trust and recognition of needs are part of any transactional, consultative, or enterprise relationship between a customer and a supplier, but the processes associated with the concepts differ according to the type of relationship sought by the partners.

Companies are continually looking for significant growth opportunities within current accounts. In a Gallup survey of salespeople, more than 60 percent reported that it took only one or two calls to consummate a sale with existing customers, but only 18 percent reported making a sale to new customers with a minimum number of calls.[1] A classic study of the relationship between the amount of time spent calling on accounts and sales performance found that only the time spent with established accounts—not new prospects—had a positive impact on sales.[2]

As we will see, relationship management includes knowledge of the typical stages in the B2B purchasing process and the various types of account relationships within each stage. Managers are also familiar with the concept of a buying center, the development of selling teams, and other steps distributors can take to ensure profitable account relationships.

PURCHASING PROCESS

To be successful, the distributor sales force must create value for the customer. It is important to understand that distributors can add value along various points in the purchasing process. Typically, there are four steps that purchasers take as they move through a B2B client acquisition (Figure 1).[3] This process can take up to a year, especially when large projects overhaul aspects of a customer's organizational infrastructure, such as manufacturing or information systems. Sometimes, the customer's purchasing department has little or no involvement in a customer's strategic purchases.

---

[1] Allison Lucas, "Leading Edge," *Sales & Sales Management* (June 1995), p. 13.
[2] William Weeks and Lynn Kahle, "Salespeople's Time Use and Performance," *Journal of Personal Selling & Sales Management* (Winter 1990), pp. 29–37.
[3] For further information about the purchasing process, see Alston Gardner, Stephen Bistritz, and Jay Klompmaker, "Selling to Senior Executives," Marketing Management (Summer 1998), pp. 11–20.

Recognition of Needs

The first stage of *need recognition occurs* when the account (i.e., customer) recognizes that a need exists. In some cases, the need is immediate and focuses on resolving a problem, such as a bottleneck in the production process or a breakdown of machinery. This type of need is typical of a transactional relationship.

Figure 1
The Purchasing Process

Sales Force Role

| Help customers recognize a need or problem. Redefine issues in a new way. | Identify viable alternative solutions. Effectively deal with uncertainty. | Help expedite the purchase process. Make it convenient and uncomplicated. | Support decisions through post-sale service. Demonstrate product. |

In a consultative selling relationship, a customer may not be aware of the nature or extent of a problem or opportunity. Transcend Services, Inc. of Atlanta, Georgia, creates selling opportunities by conducting operational assessments of hospital medical records departments. The company analyses how a department's processes and procedures work, and how well it adheres to performance standards and interfaces with the rest of the hospital. If the audit indicates that cost savings are feasible within predetermined performance standards, the company develops a proposal for taking over management of the hospital's records department (including redeploying hospital employees as Transcend employees). According to Transcend's president and CEO, Larry Gerdes, an audit may take two to three days to perform, the report takes an additional week to complete, and the entire purchasing process typically takes about six months. But the strategy allows Transcend to gain customers by helping them understand and quantify the magnitude of their problems.

To recognize B2B buying needs, salespeople should understand the concept of *derived demand*. As we have seen, professional buyers in the distribution industry do not purchase for themselves; they buy products to resell, or buy products to fabricate or kit and then resell. Derived demand is the demand for a product that results from the demand for the customer's products. Suppliers can gain a competitive advantage by knowing and understanding the needs of their customers' customers. Derived demand may influence who the sales force calls on, what customer benefits are emphasized, and how much of a product or service is ultimately sold. For example, to increase demand from their distributors, manufacturer salespeople often demonstrate the advantages of their products to business customers that buy from their distributors. Their reasoning is that increased customer demand will help convince distributors to increase purchases of that product line; they "sell" their products to distributors by selling the product to the end users.

Evaluation of Options

For some companies, purchased materials may represent as much as 80 percent of an original equipment manufacturer's (OEM) total product costs. Since a mistake in selecting a supplier could be disastrous, businesses spend considerable time and money searching for and evaluating suppliers according to the strategic significance of their purchases.[4] As we have seen, Mayer Electric Supply devoted extensive resources to winning its contract with ThyssenKrupp, but most purchasers do not have the capability to establish this type of working relationship with all their suppliers. When information needs are minimal, or the impact of the purchase on the organization is low, companies are likely to base their supplier selection on a catalog search or automatic reorder from a favored supplier. Thus, it is important to understand the customer's situation with respect to both costs and opportunities at this phase of the purchasing process.

---

[4] Jan Heide and Allen Weiss, "Vendor Consideration and Switching Behavior for Buyers in High Technology Markets," *Journal of Marketing* (July 1995), pp. 30–43.

Specifications. One of the key activities of the *evaluation of options* phase is the development of a precise statement of requirements and tolerances, known as "product specifications." Anticipated demand for an organization's products and the technological requirements of its operations determine exact specifications. This stage is often critical for potential suppliers because final specifications will also determine the cost to produce the product and can favor one supplier's product over another. By getting involved in this phase of the process, suppliers significantly increase their chances of being selected.

In most transactional-type relationships, customers develop their own product specifications without the involvement of a supplier. In consultative and enterprise-type relationships, however, customers and suppliers tend to work together to develop product specifications. For example, DaimlerChrysler chose Johnson Controls, Inc. to supply seats for one of its models. Johnson was able to meet the customer's cost target but fell far short on safety, weight, and comfort. A team of ten Chrysler engineers, led by the sales director, met with ten Johnson counterparts. After five long days, they agreed on weight, cost, and performance targets and worked together to help Johnson meet the targets.[5] In more advanced buyer–seller relationships, such as the association between Johnson Controls and DaimlerChrysler, close collaboration between the supplier and customer may lead to the selection of the supplier well before the supplier bid process takes place.

Sales Proposal. A *sales proposal* is a seller's written offer to provide a product or service to a purchasing organization. The proposal may represent the culmination of several months of extensive client analysis, or it may result from receiving a *request for proposal (RFP)* from a buyer. An RFP is a notice that a customer sends to qualified suppliers inviting them to bid on a project within a certain set of specifications. It is important for suppliers to integrate the proposal development process into the selling process. When purchasing materials and equipment, for example, building contractors may consider service, quality of product, supplier support, price, and reputation for fair dealing to be among their most important criteria for choosing suppliers; the relative importance of these criteria may vary between contractors. The proposal is the outcome of the first two

---

[5] Tim Minahan, "Chrysler Elects Procurement Team Leader as Its New President," *Purchasing Magazine* (January 1998), pp. 22–25.

phases of the purchasing process: identification of needs and evaluation of options.

Purchase Decision

Businesses with extensive buying experience of a particular product will approach the purchase decision differently than those with limited buying experience. As a result, most B2B buying models focus on the "buying situation" rather than on products. There are three commonly recognized B2B buying situations: (1) new task, (2) modified rebuy, and (3) straight rebuy. Both the purchasing process and the selling approach differ, according to the buying situation.

New Task. A *new task* buying situation is a purchasing decision that involves significant uncertainty, with little or no previous buying experiences; purchasers need a lot of information to explore ways to solve their problem. When confronted with a new task buying situation, buyers tend to use extensive problem solving skills, because they lack a strong predisposition toward a particular result. For example, first-time buyers of complex production equipment may not be sure of which brand to select, the level of quality needed in the equipment, or how much to pay for the product. In this situation, making a wrong decision could have adverse financial and strategic implications.

> ***Recommendations to Selling Firms:*** To increase the odds of being selected as the supplier in a new task buy, the selling team should participate in the initial stages of the purchase process. For example, the sales team could gather information on the reasons for the need to buy the product, co-create the specific product specifications, and present proposals to meet the requirements.

Selling firms that are already supplying other products to the organization ("in" suppliers) have a tremendous advantage over other firms. The sales team is better equipped to understand the issues that created the need for purchasing the product, and it is familiar with the culture and behavioral history of the organization. By carefully monitoring the changing needs of the organization and being available and willing to assist, selling firms significantly enhance their chances of being selected by new task buyers.

Modified rebuy. In a *modified rebuy* situation, buyer purchasing agents believe they can generate significant benefits by reevaluating alternative solutions. Although the buyers have experience in purchasing a product, they believe it is worthwhile to seek additional information about alternative solutions and vendors. Several factors may contribute to a buyer's decision to reclassify a routine purchase into a modified rebuy. The buyer may have a renewed internal focus on quality improvements or cost reductions, or an "out" supplier may offer other quality, cost, or service improvements. Most often, however, a modified rebuy situation occurs when the firm is displeased with the timely service and performance of the present supplier.

> *Recommendations to Selling Firms:* Appropriate selling firm actions depend on whether the firm is an "in" or "out" supplier. "In" suppliers should make maximum effort to completely understand and satisfy both the explicit (stated) and implicit (implied) buyer needs. The goal is to reinforce the buyer's purchase decisions by acting quickly to provide information that will sufficiently answer their questions. In this way, the seller can convert the purchasing decision back to a straight rebuy.
>
> The goal of the "out" supplier is to keep the buying firm in the modified rebuy stage long enough for the buyer to evaluate an alternative product. Offering a performance guarantee as part of the proposal is a particularly effective "out" supplier strategy.[6] For example, guaranteeing "next day or it's free" is likely to prompt a switch from a current "in" supplier with a poor record of on-time delivery.

Straight rebuy. In a *straight rebuy* situation, the buyer has had substantial experience in buying the product, requires little or no new information, and does not require any changes in the product or the offering. Typically, a buyer needs to replenish inventories of frequently purchased products, with no modification of specifications. The buyer's purchase decisions are limited to quantity and the delivery timetable. In this case, the seller can deliver value to the customer by

---

[6] Mary Seigfried Dozbaba, "Critical Supplier Relationships: Converting Higher Performance," *Purchasing Today* (February 1999): pp. 22-29.

making the purchase easy, convenient, and hassle-free. Salespeople with long-term customer relationships may even save the customer time by writing the purchase orders themselves.

Companies are increasingly requiring their suppliers to support just-in-time inventory practices, improve supply chain management, and furnish instant order status information through *extranets*. Extranets link trading partners' computer networks via the Internet to provide a secure private electronic environment for real-time communication. By connecting with the customer's computer system and accessing a distributor's inventory information, a supplier can automatically ship products for inventory replenishment. The Dutch brewing company Heineken recently initiated a system that allows its 450 distributors to forecast and order online, reducing order cycle time from three months to four weeks.[7]

Marshall Industries, a leading distributor of steel products, has gone one step further with its extranet, allowing customers to track order status, expedite shipping by linking to freight forwarders, participate in live engineering seminars with video and audio, and get live, online support.

Recommendations to Selling Firms: Once again, selling firm actions depend on whether the firm is an "in" or "out" supplier. The "in" supplier should reinforce the value of the current relationship, continue to meet the buying firm's expectations, and constantly monitor the landscape for changing needs of the organization. Buyers are not always looking for the lowest prices; some realize that they can work more efficiently with key suppliers to satisfy the needs of the end consumer, at a lower overall cost. Grief Brothers Corporation, manufacturer of fiber and plastic drums, routinely conducts "cost-in-use" studies to document the incremental cost savings that accrue to customers who choose the company's higher cost products and services over less expensive alternatives. A Grief technical service manager works with customer managers to estimate the customer's current total costs and identify system solutions (just-in-time deliveries, a new delivery system, drum recycling). By presenting their customers with a variety of service alternatives, along with estimates of cost savings, Grief helps its clients make more informed purchase

---

[7] Mary Shoemaker, "A Framework for Examining IT-enabled Market Relationships," *Journal of Personal Selling & Sales Management*, 21 (Spring 2001), p. 178.

decisions, based on the total worth of system solutions.[8]

Information gathering is critical to the success of the "out" supplier. The "out" supplier has to convince the buyer, with sufficient information, that organizational requirements have changed and that the buyer should interpret them differently. This is not an easy task, as buyers tend to perceive vendor switching as a risky practice. If the "out" supplier is unsuccessful in reducing the customer's perceived risk, it is likely that the customer will continue to regard vendor switching as time consuming and unnecessary. The selling firm's objective is to gather enough evidence to persuade the buyer to reexamine alternative solutions and revise the preferred supplier list to include the seller as a new supplier.

Post-Sale Evaluation

Closing the sale is only the beginning of the relationship in most B2B selling situations. The seller's primary responsibility following the purchase is to ensure it fulfills all promises and meets or exceeds all customer expectations. This assurance includes making sure the product has no defects and that it arrives on time, to the right location. Additional service responsibilities include expediting any needed repairs or exchanges, honoring warranties quickly and smoothly, and providing adequate customer training.

Despite the seller's best efforts, conflicts are likely to arise. Some have argued that conflict management is the key competency of salespeople who succeed in sustaining a B2B partnership.[9] Research suggests that effectively managed conflict can have a positive effect on relationships and sales. Some of the potential benefits include (1) stimulating interest in exploring new approaches, (2) providing an opportunity to air problems and explore solutions, and (3) mobilizing the resources of the parties in a relationship.[10]

Many customer organizations evaluate their suppliers and the products they buy by using a value analysis or a vendor analysis. *Value analysis,* developed by

---

[8] James Anderson and James Narus, *Business Market Management* (Upper Saddle River, NJ: Prentice-Hall, 1999), pp. 172–173.
[9] Barton Weitz and Kevin Bradford, "Personal Selling and Sales Management: A Relationship Marketing Perspective," *Journal of the Academy of Marketing Science,* 27, 2 (1999), pp. 241–254.
[10] Louis Stern, Adel El-Ansary, and Anne Coughlan, *Marketing Channels* (Upper Saddle River, NJ: Prentice-Hall, 1996).

General Electric Company as a basis for cost reduction, is a detailed analysis of a product that calculates its total cost. Components of total product cost include possession costs (related to holding inventory) and acquisition costs (associated with originating requisitions, interviewing salespeople, expediting deliveries, receiving and editing invoices, and following up on inaccurate and late deliveries). These costs usually far exceed the invoice price that the customer pays for the product. Value analysis therefore determines the relative cost of providing a necessary function or service at the desired time and place with the necessary quality.

Vendor analysis focuses on the supplier company by looking at items such as delivery reliability and timeliness, service quality, warranty support, supplier communication, and technical competence. For example, Deere & Company calculates a measure of "wavelength," using values such as attitude, responsiveness, and follow-up on details—information that is seldom communicated but important to track in today's competitive markets.[11]

Supplier Tiers

Organizations recognize that some suppliers are much more important to their success than are other suppliers. As a result, companies develop *supplier tiers* based on the importance of the supplier's product and the difficulty of finding alternative sources for the product.[12] Relationship investments and purchasing processes differ according to the tier of the supplier; firms devote more time and effort to top-tier category relationships than to the lower tiers. There are many products and services (for which there are many qualified suppliers) that make little difference to the quality of an organization's offering; in these cases, procurement cost containment and maintenance of a reliable source of supplies take priority. Note that the practice of supplier tiering mirrors a supplier's account relationship strategy. As more companies realize the competitive advantages of tiering, it becomes even more important for suppliers to develop and execute a clear account relationship strategy.

Allocating the right amount of selling investment effort to each type of

---

[11] Jim Morgan, "Top Execs Pinpoint Six Game-Changing Strategies," *Velocity* (2nd Quarter 2001), p. 48.
[12] Jeffrey Dyer, Dong Cho, and Wujin Chu, "Strategic Supplier Segmentation," *California Management Review*, 40, (Winter 1998), pp 57–77.

customer relationship requires a high degree of customer intimacy; salespeople need to be aware of the customer's problems and priorities, expectations, needs, and culture.[13] It is incumbent upon the sales force to know the identity and roles of the customer personnel involved in the purchasing decision. This knowledge is particularly important in complex sales situations, such as new task and modified rebuy purchases, in which several people in the customer's organization are required to give their approval before the sale can take place. As we will see, the added complexity of selling to more than one person in an organization requires a special framework.

BUYING CENTER

A *buying center* consists of all personnel who are formally or informally involved in the purchasing decision—everyone that must say "yes" for a sale to occur or that influences the people who will ultimately make a decision about the purchase. Buying centers are not usually formal departments; they may change over time and according to product type. The number of people included in the buying center may vary from one to six or more, depending on factors such as the number of departments using the item, its strategic importance to the company, the dollar value of the purchase, and the product's degree of technical sophistication. For example, a company buying new, unfamiliar pieces of office equipment may have a purchasing agent, an office manager, a controller, and a department supervisor who will use the equipment. Each staff member will have unique purchasing criteria when selecting an office equipment supplier. The concept of the buying center is critical for salespeople to understand; many people with distinct priorities, perspectives, and personalities are likely to be involved in the purchasing process, and the salesperson must deal with each of these people individually to accomplish a successful sale.

Purchasing decision makers play specific roles within a buying center. These roles typically fall into four categories: (1) decision makers, (2) users, (3) gatekeepers and (4) advocates. A buying center member may occupy multiple purchasing roles, but one individual typically holds at least one role during any

---

[13] See Arun Sharma and Rajnandini Pillai, "Customers' Decision-Making Styles and the Preferences for Sales Strategies: Conceptual Examination and Empirical Study," *Journal of Personal Selling & Sales Management*, 16 (Winter 1996), pp. 21–34.

Account Relationship Management

major purchase.[14] To successfully conclude the sale, a fourth person must also be present; this person is referred to as an advocate.

Decision Makers

The *decision maker* is the staff member or committee with the power to give final approval to purchase the product or service. Decision makers have access to the funds necessary to make the purchase and the authority to enter into an agreement, should they choose to do so. They focus on not only price and technology but also on performance—what the organization gets in return for spending money. Decision makers also:

- Focus on the future.
- Establish the priority of projects.
- Can say "yes" even if everyone else says "no."
- Can say "no" when everyone else says "yes."[15]

For each sale, it is crucial to identify the decision makers. In complex, strategically important purchases, they are usually near the top of the organizational ladder, but their exact position will depend on a number of factors. Top-rung decision makers are more likely to be involved when:

- The product is more expensive.
- The organization's business conditions are more depressed.
- The customer has less experience with the supplier and the supplier's product.
- There will be a greater negative impact if the organization makes the wrong purchase decision.

---

[14] This discussion is based on concepts presented in Stephen Heiman, Diane Sanchez, Tad Tuleja, and Robert Miller, *The New Strategic Selling* (New York: Morrow, 1998), pp. 81–115.
[15] Mark Shonka and Dan Kosch, *Beyond Selling Value* (Chicago, IL: Dearborn Trade Publications, 2002), p.58.

Account Relationship Management

Salespeople can use the following series of questions to identify decision makers:

- Who else is involved in making the purchase decision?
- Who initiated the project?
- Who will be most affected by the outcome of the project?
- Who stands to gain the most if the project succeeds?
- Who has the highest rank and the greatest influence?

Users

The role of *users* is to determine how the proposed product or service will affect the job that they or their co-workers perform. Users have a narrower focus than decision makers do, because they are concerned primarily with their own operating areas or departments. Users are:

- Directly affected by the product or service.
- Concerned with implementation issues.
- Oriented to tactical rather than strategic views.
- Focused on the past and present rather than the future, except to ask, "How will this affect me?"

Users want to know how the supplier's solution will affect them; they are less likely to be concerned with how the solution affects the company. Nevertheless, users may represent a very powerful buying influence that is important for the seller to identify. The famous story of 3M's Post-it® notes illustrates this point: Initial efforts to sell the stick-on notes to office managers met with little success, but when the company gave free samples to secretaries and office workers, the product took off.

Sometimes it is difficult to identify the buying influence of users. For example, truck axle sales involve at least three sets of users: manufacturing engineers who design manufacturing processes, assembly plant workers who fit the axle onto the truck, and, ultimately, the customer who buys the truck. This user complexity increases the number of people and issues that supplier salespeople must address.

Gatekeepers

During the purchase decision process, *gatekeepers* screen out products and suppliers that do not meet the buying organization's requirements. Their job is to narrow down the supplier choices to alternatives that are most likely to fulfill their purchase objectives. By deciding which suppliers are included as finalists, gatekeepers have a powerful influence on the buying process. Purchasing agents often act as gatekeepers. They focus on the quantifiable aspects of the product or service as they relate to the specifications. However, depending on the complexity of the product, other buying center members, such as engineers or legal counsel, may perform this function. (In truck axle sales, for example, product engineers and designers assume the role.)

Sometimes gatekeepers can confuse salespeople by taking on the appearance of decision makers. This may occur when gatekeepers attempt to elevate their perceived importance within the organization. Salespeople may be misled, and as a result, the sale may go to the competitor that identified and dealt with the actual decision maker.

Gatekeepers have the ability to control the flow of information, so it is critical for salespeople to understand why a gatekeeper might block the completion of a sale. Their reasons for thwarting sales efforts could include underestimating the seller's value to their organization, having a bias toward other competitors, or attempting to maintain personal control over the purchasing process. Each of these situations calls for a different sales strategy. Gatekeepers' motivations are often emotionally charged; dealing effectively with them requires salespeople to have a high level of emotional intelligence. [16]

Despite their frustrations with gatekeepers, salespeople must acknowledge that they serve an important function in the buying center. Gatekeepers are diligent about finding the greatest value to their firm—the lowest price, the products or services with required specifications, the best service plan, or some combination of all three features. Gatekeepers also safeguard the valuable time of top-level executives. When dealing with gatekeepers, it may be useful for salespeople to remember the old saying, "Don't ever slam the door, you might want to go back." In summary, a gatekeeper may:

---

[16] For an excellent discussion of assessing the blocking actions of gatekeepers and developing strategies for overcoming these actions, see Shonba and Kosch. *Beyond Selling Value*, pp. 148–163.

- Be able to say "no" but need to get approval before saying "yes."
- Be able to recommend.
- Be a key influence on the decision maker.
- Be concerned about product specifications and financials.

Advocates

An *advocate* helps a salesperson by providing important information about the people involved in the purchase decision and the organization. These people may be internal or external to the buying organization and do not necessarily make the sale or make referrals, but they are willing to provide key information about those who do exert influence. They are often able to speak on behalf of the seller when the seller is absent (e.g., during purchasing committee meetings). Advocates are motivated to assist the salesperson when they are convinced that the seller's product is best for the organization and have a personal interest in ensuring the sale. Advocates may want to help for the following reasons:

- *Professional:* To meet company performance objectives and politically enhance their careers by advocating for a particular vendor.
- *Personal:* To help a supplier win because they know and like the salesperson and want to see the salesperson succeed.
- *Recognition:* To receive organizational recognition by successfully advocating for the winning supplier.
- *Negative:* To ensure that someone else loses.[17]

To help ensure a sale, advocates can:

- *Act as reviewers:* Go over selling materials to ensure that the seller has prioritized the right areas, used correct terms, and picked up the nuances of the buying center.
- *Recommend specific strategies:* Clarify each buying center member's priorities, identify decision makers, and highlight key organizational issues.

---

[17] Mark Shonka and Dan Kosch, *Beyond Selling Value* (Chicago, IL: Dearborn Trade Publications, 2002), p. 58.

Account Relationship Management

- *Manage and direct discussion:* Encourage and manage types of discussions among decision influencers.
- *Provide references:* Identify other advocates in the company who may be interested in the seller's success.
- *Gain access to decision makers:* Obtain access to the executive suite.

Before selecting an advocate, it is important for salespeople to do their homework; they should seek a contact that buying center members regard as trustworthy and competent. To identify the appropriate person, salespeople should pay special attention to the name that buying center members most frequently mention; members are likely to recognize an advocate selected in this way as a group leader and influencer. It is important to have a strong advocate; when a decision maker publicly states a position about a seller ("I do not think this supplier would meet our needs"), it is very difficult to change the decision maker's mind. In such cases, only a respected advocate can make a compelling argument on behalf of the seller.

RELATIONSHIP BUILDING

Although there is debate about the profitability that long-term customers provide to an organization,[18] most salespeople work to establish strong customer relationships that ensure a stream of future purchases and provide further cross-selling and up-selling opportunities. Many companies depend on their salespeople to build and enhance professional relationships at all levels in the organization. It is helpful to understand how relationships evolve over time.

How Relationships Evolve

According to social psychology research, B2B relationships evolve through five general stages: (1) awareness, (2) exploration, (3) expansion, (4) commitment, and (5) dissolution.[19] Each stage represents a significant shift in selling opportunities. Salespeople must be aware of the changes occurring in the relationship and

---

[18] Werner Reinartz and V. Kumar, "The Mismanagement of Customer Loyalty," *Harvard Business Review,* (July, 2002), pp. 4 – 12.
[19] James C. Anderson, "Relationships in Business Markets: Exchange Episodes, Value Creation, and Their Empirical Assessment," *Journal of the Academy of Marketing Science,* 23 (1996), pp. 346–350.

proceed accordingly. Figure 2 summarizes the five stages of *relationship evolution* and the objectives associated with each stage. Relationships tend to evolve in a dynamic, rather than linear, fashion, cycling through the various stages shown in Figure 2. Committed B2B relationships often re-enter the exploration phase to find new opportunities to create customer value. In these situations, working together on a common goal raises the level of relationship commitment.

Figure 2
Buyer–Seller Relationship Stages

Relationship Stage	Description	Key Selling Objectives
Awareness	Recognition that a supplier may be able to satisfy an important need.	1. Gain customer's attention. 2. Demonstrate how the product or service can satisfy a need.
Exploration	A trial order with limited commitments by both parties. The trial period may continue for an extended period.	1. Gain initial acceptance. 2. Build a successful relationship.
Expansion	Expansion of rewards for each party in the relationship.	1. Gain better understanding of the customer's business. 2. Expand ways to help the customer.
Commitment	The buyer and seller are committed to an exclusive relationship.	1. Ensure that buying and selling organizations interact at multiple levels. 2. Ensure that the supplier is involved in problem solving processes at an early stage. 3. Ensure that the relationship has a long-term focus.
Dissolution	Total disengagement from the relationship. This may occur at any point in the relationship.	1. Look for warning signals. 2. Attempt to reinitiate the relationship.

Account Relationship Management

Dissolving a relationship is never easy. The process often creates ill will between two companies. However, there are cases in which the dissolution of customer relationships actually created stronger relationship commitments. In one case, an Asian competitor to a large North American petrochemical supplier offered lower prices to the supplier's customers. The North American supplier, in a carefully calculated move, decided not to counter the offer for three of its largest, but most unprofitable, customers. The supplier's decision to let go of the three customers rested on its knowledge of the new competitor's weakness: It was confident that the Asian company would not be able to deliver. As it turned out, two of the three defecting customers returned to the North American supplier after just two months of coping with the competitor's poor logistics and even poorer product quality. In fact, they accepted higher net prices and longer, guaranteed-volume deals.[20]

RELATIONSHIP BINDERS

There are three underlying factors necessary for a fully developed relationship that every salesperson and marketer should know and understand: building trust, creating value, and meeting expectations.[21] These factors are known as *relationship binders*.

Building Trust

In our context, *trust* is the belief that an individual's word or promise is dependable and that the individual will serve the long-term interests of the customer. A salesperson earns trust over time; it is an essential building block for establishing a high-quality working partnership. In many cases, the salesperson represents the company's brand in the minds of the customer, and it is often difficult for a customer to differentiate between their feelings about the supplier and their

---

[20] John Abele, Brian Elliott, Ann O'Hara, and Eric Roegner, "Fighting for Your Price," *McKinsey Quarterly*, 4 (2002), p. 21.
[21] For more on relationship binders, see David T. Wilson, "An Integrated Model of Buyer-Seller Relationships," *Journal of the Academy of Marketing Science*, 23 (1996), pp. 225–245.

feelings about the salesperson.[22] Research suggests that customer trust in the supplier's salesperson is particularly important in growing the relationship past the exploration phase.[23]

According to research that investigates buyer and seller relationships, the five most important trust-earning attributes of salespeople include:

- *Dependability:* Following through on promises.
- *Competence:* Knowing what they are talking about.
- *Customer Orientation:* Putting buyers' interests ahead of their own.
- *Honesty:* Telling the truth.
- *Likeability:* Being someone the buyer enjoys knowing.[24]

Although most of these attributes are cognitive or rational in nature, likeability is an emotional dimension. Some studies of customer trust of salespeople indicate that likeability is the most important determinant of trust, regardless of the length or type of account relationship.

While it is difficult to trust someone who is disliked, trust building does not depend entirely on personal likability. In fact, there is evidence that people place greater trust in those whom they feel have good listening skills.[25] Fortunately, salespeople can acquire good listening skills with practice. They can paraphrase or repeat questions to gain a better understanding of the question before answering, learn to avoid interrupting the speaker and answering at the appropriate time, use complete sentences instead of saying simply "yes" or "no," and tolerate silences by

---

[22] Michael Dorsch, Scott Swanson, and Scott Kelley, "The Role of Relationship Quality in the Stratification of Vendors as Perceived by Customers," *Journal of the Academy of Marketing Science,* 26, 2 (1998), pp. 128–142.

[23] Sandy Jap, "The Strategic Role of the Salesforce in Developing Customer Satisfaction Across the Relationship Lifecycle," *Journal of Personal Selling & Sales Management,* 21 (Spring 2001), pp. 95–108.

[24] For more on building trust, see Carolyn Nicholson, Larry Compeau, and Rajesh Sethi, "The Role of Interpersonal Liking in Building Trust in Long-Term Channel Relationships, *Journal of the Academy of Marketing Science,* 29 (2001), pp. 3–15; Patricia Doney and Joseph Cannon, "An Examination of the Nature of Trust in Buyer-Seller Relationships," *Journal of Marketing,* 61 (April 1997) pp. 35–51; and Robert Morgan and Shelby Hunt, "The Commitment-Trust Theory of Relationship Marketing," *Journal of Marketing,* 58 (July 1994), pp. 20–38.

[25] Lucette Comer and Tanya Drollinger, "Active Empathetic Listening and Selling Success: A Conceptual Framework," *Journal of Personal Selling & Sales Management,* 19 (Winter 1999), pp. 15–29, and Rosemary Ramsey and Ravipreet Sohi, "Listening to Your Customers: The Impact of Perceived Salesperson Listening Behavior on Relationship Outcomes," *Journal of the Academy of Marketing Science,* 25, 2 (1997), pp. 127–137.

not feeling obligated to fill in conversation.

Creating Value

Value is an implicit calculation by a buyer that the ratio of the rewards to the costs of establishing or expanding a relationship is greater than 1. For a buyer in a B2B context, perceived value is more complex than the lowest list price. It may involve lowering total inventory costs by using just-in-time delivery, providing savings in time and labor, or driving higher sales of the customer's products. Value is demonstrated when it reaches the customer's customers in the form of less expensive products, better quality or wider choices, and quicker access to those choices.

The sales force can create customer value during each phase of the purchasing process. In transactional relationships, value-adding opportunities include making the purchase process easy and hassle-free and preventing post-sale issues. These activities occur during the final two phases of the purchase process; in consultative customer relationships, sellers create customer value in the first phases of the relationship by helping customers solve problems and identify growth opportunities. These activities require a significant investment of time and effort by the salesperson during the riskiest ("assessment of needs and alternatives") part of the sales process. There is no guarantee that the investment will pay off with a sale. In enterprise relationships, the goal is to create exceptional customer value during all four phases of the purchasing process.

Meeting Expectations

Expectations are the rules or norms associated with acceptable conduct and performance. Relational expectations vary by individual preferences, company policies, and even international cultures. For example, when dealing with Asian buyers, it is customary to spend a significant amount of time in non-business discussions prior to getting down to business.

Most relationship expectations are unwritten, but some partners involved in complex enterprise-type relationships create memorandums of understanding to make all members aware of the accepted standards of conduct. This step ensures that new members of the team can quickly understand and comply with mutual values.

In newly established relationships, salespeople often believe that price discounting is necessary to gain business. However, this practice may encourage unfavorable buyer expectations. For example, if a salesperson agrees to a special price discount at the buyer's request, the buyer may think this is standard practice and expect future discounts. One way companies deal with this issue is to refrain from giving their salespeople the flexibility to discount prices.

Expectations also develop with respect to performance. Customer performance expectations include not only the performance of the product but also service activities such as frequency of sales calls, notification of price changes, lead time in delivery, order fill rate, emergency orders, and installation. Studies comparing the performance perceptions of salespeople in a wide variety of industries show that greater ability to identify the buyer's performance expectations relates to higher sales. However, the studies also show that salespeople have inaccurate perceptions of buyers' performance expectations. Interestingly, the studies found the more experienced salespeople to be less accurate in interpreting their buyers' performance expectations.[26]

To encourage accuracy in assessing customer expectations, some companies require their salespeople to provide an annual written assessment of their key customers. This assessment process involves answering a series of questions to identify key assumptions, inconsistencies, and missing information. Figure 3 lists the types of questions that salespeople should use to assess customer accounts. The extent of the detail, depth, and complexity of the questions will undoubtedly vary with the type of relationship (transactional, consultative, or enterprise). The objective, however, is to have superior customer intelligence—better information than any competitor has about the account.

---

[26] Douglas Lambert, Howard Marmorstein, and Arun Sharma, "The Accuracy of Salespersons' Perceptions of Their Customers: Conceptual Examination and an Empirical Study," *Journal of Personal Selling & Sales Management,* (Winter 1990), pp.1-9.

Figure 3
Customer Account Information

Information Type	Examples of Customer Assessment Questions
Market	What are the important markets the customer serves? Which of the customer's products are most important in terms of revenue and profit contribution? Major competitors?
Financial	What is the projected annual capital spending amount? When does the budgeting process begin and end? Who initiates capital project requests? What financing is needed to win approval?
Organizational	What reporting relationships in each department influence purchasing decisions? What are the top business objectives that each manager must achieve?
Operational	How does the company produce results (raw materials used, equipment, budget to produce finished goods)? How does the firm evaluate products or services?
Personnel	Who has a direct or indirect influence on product buying decisions? How often has the salesperson met with them in the past year? What is the relationship with each person? Who are the salesperson's friends and enemies within the account?
Competitive	What is the account share for each competitor? Which of the competitors with an installed base position in the account is most vulnerable? Which ones are likely to gain share?

Building trust, creating value and meeting expectations are critical to establishing and building lasting customer relationships. The method of achieving these "relationship binders," the activities involved, and the skills needed to enhance them depend on the account relationship strategy. Figure 4 summarizes the differences across relationship binders, according to the three types of account relationship strategies.

Figure 4
Binding Account Relationships

	Transactional Relationship	Consultative Relationship	Enterprise Relationship
Value	Provide a good product that the buyer can purchase conveniently.	Provide a solution to an important problem.	Increase the shareholder value of the organization.
Expectations	Ensure that the buyer has a clear set of expectations about the conduct of the relationship.	Recognize that the buyer knows a problem exists but is unsure of the solution.	Recognize that the buyer's expectations are strategic in nature, though the process for achieving strategic objectives may be unknown.
Trust	Do what is promised.	Do what is necessary to solve the problem.	Do everything possible to increase the buyer's competitive advantage in the marketplace.

SUMMARY

It is critical to a supplier's profitability and growth to establish relationships with the right customers and manage each relationship to deliver value. As we have seen, there are several concepts that are important for successful account relationship management. You should now be able to:

1. Describe the steps in the professional purchasing process. There are four basic steps in the typical purchasing process: recognition of needs, evaluation of options, decision about the purchase, and post-sale evaluation. Sales forces have the opportunity to create customer value during each of these steps. However, the level of customer value created will depend on the type of buyer–supplier relationship—transactional, consultative, or enterprise.

2. Identify influences in the buying center. Several people are likely to be involved in most organizational purchasing decisions. This group is known as the buying center. It is important that salespeople identify all those involved in the center, as well as the nature of their involvement. Regardless of functional area or level in the organization, people in the buying center will assume one of three roles: decision maker, user, or gatekeeper. In addition, salespeople should choose and cultivate an advocate in the buying center.

3. Explain how relationships are likely to evolve. Relationships evolve through five general stages: (1) awareness, (2) exploration, (3) expansion, (4) commitment, and (5) dissolution. Because each stage represents a major shift in the nature of the relationship, salespeople should be aware of these changes and proceed accordingly.

4. Describe factors critical to gaining commitment to a relationship. Certain factors are important for gaining increasing levels of commitment in relationships. There are three factors necessary for establishing a fully developed and productive relationship: building trust, creating value, and meeting expectations. Each factor applies to a professional account relationship situation, and there are ways to identify and enhance the factors.

MARKETING PROMOTIONS IN DISTRIBUTION CHANNELS

LEARNING OBJECTIVES

After studying this chapter, you should be able to:

- Describe distributor support as one of the major tools in the manufacturer's promotional toolbox.
- Understand the difference between push and pull promotional strategies.
- Explain why distributors use push promotional strategies with increasing frequency, and why push strategies account for higher spending than pull strategies.
- Be familiar with the major research findings on push promotions.
- Be aware of the various types of push promotional strategies.

INTRODUCTION

Imagine this scenario: Two manufacturing managers develop identical promotional campaigns under identical market conditions with equal amounts of resources to invest. One manager involves the distributor's management team in the campaign's development, by communicating the promotional strategy and demonstrating that it will enhance manufacturer support. The other manager sends the promotional campaign directly to the distributor's salespeople without involving their management team. The outcome? The manager who lays the groundwork for distributor involvement gets dramatically better results. The lesson? Promotional campaigns stand a higher probability of being successful when the manufacturer secures cooperation from the distributor.

Manufacturers and distributors use several promotional tools to enhance product sales. The term *promotion* applies to all activities a company performs to (1) raise customer or distributor awareness of a product or brand, (2) generate sales, and (3) create brand loyalty. Classic marketing textbooks describe promotion as a mixture of personal sales, advertising, sales promotion, direct marketing, and publicity. Manufacturers use sales promotion techniques to entice distributors to sell their products, even though distributors depend on those products to make a profit. Distributors are independent companies that typically carry multiple product lines from competing manufacturers; manufacturers have limited control over the efforts distributors make to promote their products. Manufacturers that use promotional tools to coax distributors to focus on their products will gain competitive advantages and receive healthy returns on their investments.

The business-to-business (B2B) environment uses two promotional strategies: pull and push. Manufacturers use the *pull strategy* to secure distributor cooperation by "pulling" their products through the channel. By advertising their products directly to end users, manufacturers force distributors to promote their products, because it is in the distributors' best interests. Auto manufacturer advertisements are examples of the pull strategy. Auto dealers reap the benefits of increased sales, which in turn requires them to order more vehicles from the manufacturers. Similarly, television ads for prescription drugs entice consumers to ask their doctors to prescribe particular brands. Although pull strategies can be effective, they are limited in their ability to secure strong distributor support. It is more effective for a manufacturer to work directly with a distributor to implement a promotional campaign.

Unlike the pull strategy, the *push strategy* requires direct involvement from the distributor. A push strategy is a promotional program offered by a manufacturer that induces support for the manufacturer's product. The manufacturer seeks the distributor's cooperation to develop and implement the promotional strategy. Successful push strategies do not force or "backdoor" a campaign onto a distributor's sales force. Figure 1 illustrates the differences between the pull and push promotional approaches.

Figure 1
Pull versus Push Promotional Strategies

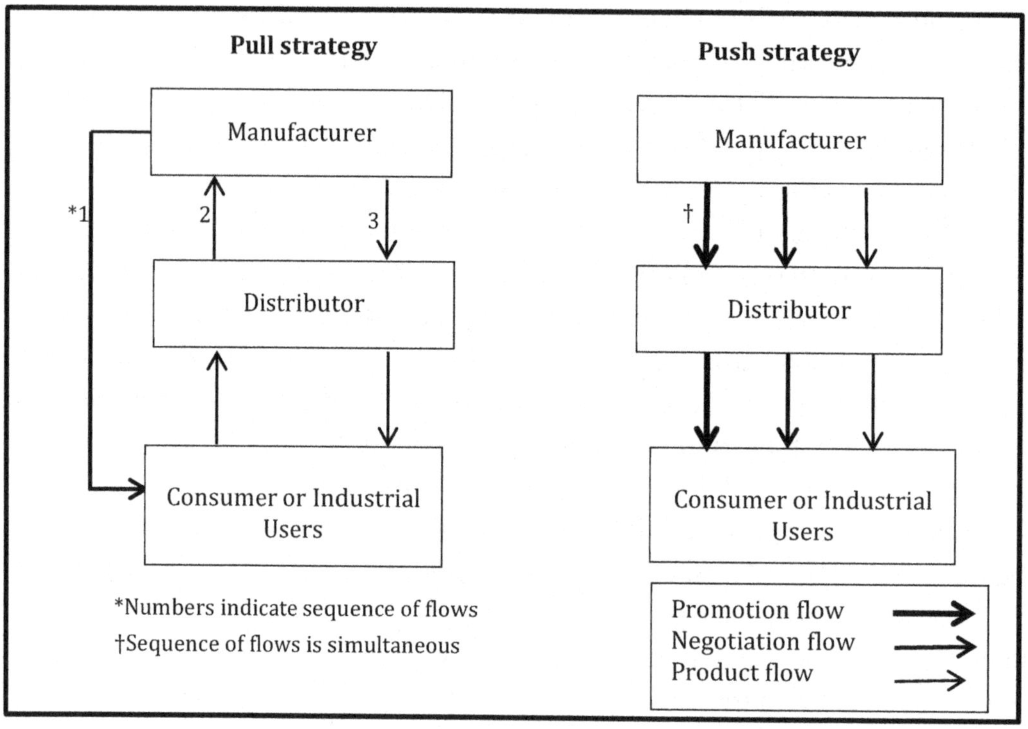

*Numbers indicate sequence of flows
†Sequence of flows is simultaneous

Promotion flow →
Negotiation flow →
Product flow →

As we will see, most of the promotional spending expended by B2B firms is devoted to push-related campaigns.

Promotional Allowances

There are many types of promotional allowances available to distributors. Most often, however, manufacturers offer cash payments or percentage discounts on particular products for a specified time. To encourage distributors to buy more of their products, manufacturers typically tie allowances and discounts to a specific volume of purchases. Distributors respond by giving the products prominent wholesale or retail shelf space, featuring the products in training and staff meetings, and developing incentive programs for their own sales forces. Although some members of the industry question the ethical status of allowances, others regard them as legitimate costs of doing business.

The use of promotional allowances has been growing in recent years. However, they can become very expensive for manufacturers, easily amounting to 5 percent of sales.[1] Nevertheless, manufacturers continue to use allowances because of the proliferation of products on the market and a growing reliance on distributors to market their products. It is easier and more effective for manufacturers to design promotional allowance campaigns that appeal to their distribution channel members than to develop marketing messages for end users. The key to an effective promotional campaign is to ensure that the promotional allowance program is consistent with distributor needs.[2]

One drawback of promotional allowances is that they are one of the prime causes of the *bullwhip effect*. The bullwhip effect can occur when distributors buy larger than normal quantities of a product, which, in turn, causes manufacturers to increase production to meet the demand. Downstream suppliers to the manufacturer must also increase their short-term production to keep up with the projected demand. For example, imagine that the actual customer demand for a product is 8 units. The distributor orders 12 units from the manufacturer, adding an extra 4 units to ensure ample floor stock. The manufacturer then places a bulk order with its supplier for components to make 20 units, so it can guarantee timely shipment to the distributor. Now that 20 units have been produced for a demand of only 8 units, the distributor will have to increase demand by dropping prices or finding more customers.

---

[1] Randery, T. Casear, B. and Longman, M, (2002), "Achieving Channel Excellence," *McKinsey & Company Marketing Practice Report* (June), 3.
[2] Walters, R. G. (1989), "An Empirical Investigation into Retailer Response to Manufacturer Trade Promotions," *Journal of Retailing*, (Summer), 253-272.

Cooperative Advertising

One of the most prevalent forms of promotional assistance offered by manufacturers to channel members is *cooperative advertising*. In just one quarter of 2009, for example, manufacturers that sold products through Walmart provided close to $100 million in cooperative advertising money to Walmart, and many additional millions of dollars to other large retailers such as Target, Walgreens, and CVS.[3]

A common form of co-op advertising is 50–50 cost sharing, based on a specified percentage of a retailer's purchases from a manufacturer. For example, if a distributor makes purchases of $200,000 from a manufacturer, the amount of advertising funds available to the retailer would be $6,000, when the maximum allowance is 3 percent of purchases. As part of this push strategy, the distributor receives compensation for advertising the manufacturer's brand.

Manufacturers use co-op advertising to strengthen the image of a brand and motivate quicker sales by the distributor. In their local advertising, distributors often use price to stimulate sales. Unlike manufacturers that rely solely on national advertising, distributors often have better access to local market knowledge and are better equipped to help consumers through the final steps of purchase. Manufacturers that want to exercise some level of control over a cooperative advertising campaign can supply advertising format suggestions, or even media-ready advertisements for newspapers, magazines, or broadcast media.

The effectiveness of cooperative advertising as a promotional strategy depends on the level of support offered by the distributor. The distributor must (1) have a sufficient inventory of the advertised product, (2) offer adequate point-of-purchase display, and (3) effectively administer the cooperative program provided by the manufacturer. Careless administration may result in poor channel member follow-through, or even outright abuse. For example, a distributor might bill the manufacturer for the national advertising rate, pay the local rate to the local ad agency, and pocket the difference. It may even use some of the co-op ad budget to advertise a completely different brand or product. To avoid such

---

[3] Neff, J. (November 30, 2009), "Wal-Mart Up the Ante with Brand Co-op Ads in More Ways than One," *Advertising Age*, p. 1-3.

abuses, some manufacturers have developed formal, carefully administered cooperative advertising programs that require distributors to provide clear-cut proof that they have properly spent the cooperative advertising money provided to them. In some cases, however, distributors complain that manufacturers focus disproportionally on only one product, to the exclusion of competing products. This perception of unfair focus on a particular brand, combined with the administrative burden of accounting for co-op advertising expenditures, leads to a situation in which approximately 50 percent of all co-op advertising dollars offered to channel members goes unused.[4]

Incentives and Contests

Manufacturers also use many types of incentives and contests to stimulate sales efforts. In some cases, they tie the promotion to a major event at the local, state, national, or even international level. The 3M company, for example, ran an incentive campaign involving distributors of its occupational health and safety products. The company tied the sales contest to the upcoming Olympics and provided prizes ranging from sweatshirts bearing the Olympic logo to major travel awards, based on the distributor salesperson's productivity.[5] The Olympic theme added glamour and excitement to the contest, while also generating a competitive spirit and sense of patriotism that boosted selling efforts.

Although manufacturers provide incentives, they do not regard them as "giveaways." They apply the general performance standard that $1 spent on incentives produces $4 of revenue. They also recognize that sales incentive programs can not only increase sales volumes but also find new customers, boost sales of special items, counteract seasonal sales slumps, and introduce new items to customers.

Manufacturers should be wary of hastily developed incentives and contests, because they are difficult to administer and may create ill will on the part of distributors. Manufacturer-developed programs may inadvertently foster selling behaviors that are detrimental to the distributor and its customers. For example, manufacturers may offer "push money" or exotic vacations to

---

[4] Roslow, S., Laskey, H. A. and Nicholls, J. A. F. (1993), "Enigma of Cooperative Advertising," *Journal of Business and Industrial Marketing,* 8 (2), 70-79.
[5] Rosenbloom, B. (2013), *Marketing Channels: A Management View,* South-Western Publishing, Mason, OH.

distributors that produce high sales volumes for a particular product, but some distributors may believe these practices conflict with their own customer and market strategies. For example, a distributor with a culture and reputation for serving customer needs would not want its staff to pressure customers to buy inappropriate products just to help salespeople win a contest. Distributors may also be unwilling to participate in contests that focus on products that are not strategically important to them; they want to avoid confusing their customers or damaging their relationships with other manufacturers.

Before implementing manufacturers' incentive programs, distributors should ask the following questions: Is the program (and the manufacturer's brand) consistent with the overall marketing strategy? Is there a possibility that the program will detract from long-run customer developmental efforts? Can the salesperson understand the incentive goals and actually reach the goals? Can the distributor measure achievement of the goals? The answers to these questions should determine a distributor's level of comfort with the proposed contest. At the same time, manufacturers should make every attempt to consider channel members' perspectives regarding contests and incentive programs. By doing so, they are more likely to avoid conflict and get buy-in from channel members.

Manufacturer incentives and contests may not always be effective in driving distributor sales. Research suggests there can be negative outcomes when making these types of trade deals. Incentives may (1) foster deal-to-deal purchasing by channel members, (2) reduce consumer brand loyalty, (3) fail to provide pass-through savings for consumers, and (4) encourage the diversion of discounted merchandise from consumers to other channel members. Failure to pass on savings to consumers is of particular concern; estimates are that only 30 percent of distributors pass manufacturer-induced trade promotion discounts through to consumers in the form of lower prices. Of the remaining 70 percent, 35 percent is lost in inefficiencies, and the other 35 percent goes directly into channel members' pockets.[6]

Promotional deals can also create a culture in which discount-driven distributors buy far more product than they can sell in a reasonable time. This practice of *forward buying*, also known as *channel stuffing*, is a prime cause of the bullwhip effect in supply chains.

---

[6] Foust, D. (December 9, 2002), "Coke: The Cost of Babying Bottlers," *Business Week*, 93-94.

There is no simple solution to the problems created by promotional deals, and there is no end in sight for incentive programs. They are part of the competitive landscape of manufacturing and distributing.

In-Store Displays and Selling Aids

The range of in-store displays and selling aids includes any type of manufacturer-provided signs, displays, racks, shelving, platforms, promotional kits, and interactive electronic displays that can be used by inside salespeople to promote the sale of products to customers. Manufacturers spend billions of dollars each year on such point of purchase (POP) displays. Although displays and selling aids can be highly effective, manufacturers can find it difficult to convince distributors to use these materials.[7] Distributors are often flooded with product display requests. For example, supermarkets receive over 1,000 promotional displays per year but have the capacity to set up only about 50 end-of-aisle displays each week. Some manufacturers recognize this problem and offer some type of special incentive (promotional allowance) to encourage the use of their materials.

Another popular form of selling aid is the "in-store" promotion event. Typically, the manufacturer sets up booths at distributor locations and provides demonstrations and hands-on training for customers. This approach is particularly useful when the manufacturer has a new line of products to introduce. Companies are finding increasingly creative ways to provide such product demonstrations; appearances by celebrities, for example, have been used to drive additional foot traffic to a store.

In-store displays and selling aids will continue to be popular in the distribution industry. Channel managers, however, must constantly monitor and evaluate the usefulness of these promotional tools.

Training Programs

One of the most effective ways for manufacturers to build the promotional support of distributors is to provide distributor salespeople with product-specific training. Product training demonstrates the manufacturer's commitment to sales success.

---

[7] Ouwarkerk, C. Verbeke, W., Hovingh, H. and Pellen, E. (1997), "Retailers' and Manufacturers' Perceptions of the Temporary Display," *Journal of Marketing Channels,* 6(1), 1-16.

Distributors value the assistance because their day-to-day demands leave them little time for product training. Small distributors and wholesalers are particularly appreciative because they do not have large training budgets, but even larger distributors enjoy manufacturers' financial assistance regard these programs as valuable supplements. From the manufacturers' perspective, distributor training increases the chances that salespeople will emphasize the manufacturers' products over other products, resulting in enhanced channel equity with the distributor.

Although product training focuses mostly on product knowledge, manufacturers also know that general selling and relationship-building skills are critical for success. Some manufacturers include other topics in their courses, such as listening, trust building, selling adaptability, and non-verbal communication. There is anecdotal evidence to suggest that expanding training programs to include selling and relationship topics results in greater salesperson loyalty; it signals that the manufacturer is concerned not only about the bottom line, but about overall salesperson excellence.

Missionary Sales Activities

Instead of selling directly (taking orders), a *manufacturer missionary* stimulates product sales by performing relationship-building activities and offering detailed product knowledge to distributor sales staff. Pharmaceutical drug representatives, for example, build brand image for their products by explaining their drugs' efficacies to doctors, answering doctors' questions, and ensuring doctors have adequate supplies. Drug reps are not responsible for closing sales, but they must have excellent product knowledge and be able to answer doctors' queries in a convincing manner. When drug reps are successful in their communications, doctors will favor the prescription of their drugs. Missionary salespeople can be valuable assets for a manufacturer when they perform the following activities:

- Travel with the distributor salesperson on sales calls to assist in selling efforts.
- Provide technical assistance.
- Train distributor salespeople.
- Assist in closing a sale that requires specific, in-depth product knowledge.
- Introduce new products.

Some industrial manufacturers use their missionary sales forces to call directly on customers. For example, though Thomas and Betts, an electrical equipment manufacturer, still relies on its distributor salespeople to close its sales, the company recently initiated a missionary sales program to develop the brand in the minds of their customers. Its sales missionaries are responsible for building relationships that encourage customers to request Thomas and Betts products when they are in need of new electrical equipment. The company's missionary salesperson experiment is working well; customers appreciate the interaction, and distributor sales reps appreciate the increased sales.

There are drawbacks to having a missionary sales force. First, some distributors may regard missionary salespeople as a waste of their already-scarce selling time. When they are selling multiple product lines in a single sales call, they may find it awkward to bring along a missionary sales rep whose products are only a small part of the overall product mix. Second, the hiring, training, and support of missionary sales forces are expensive activities; a B2B missionary sales force requires personnel with advanced education (technical or graduate degrees) and special training. Third, missionary salespeople may create channel conflict by performing tasks normally completed by distributor salespeople. A distributor could infer that the manufacturer is about to cut the distributor out, by positioning itself to sell directly. The distributor might retaliate by reducing cooperation with missionary reps and withdrawing from the manufacturer's promotional campaigns.

Trade Shows

Trade shows are important promotional opportunities for distributors to display technological advances in the industry and reinforce the benefits of existing products. Participating companies present their products and services in booths visited by industry members. Professional industry associations usually organize the shows and hold them annually or bi-annually. For example, the National Association of Electrical Distributors (NAED, www.naed.org) holds its annual meeting in early spring and runs a number of other regional and specialty conferences throughout the year. Most companies attend trade shows to identify decision influencers and potential customers; provide product, service, and company information; learn about competitive products; make actual sales; and handle current customer or supplier problems. Manufacturers use the trade show opportunity to meet with their top distributors to discuss past performance, forecast future sales, and identify new opportunities to enhance their relationships. Trade shows also enhance sales force morale when they take place in larger cities with extra activities available during non-working hours.

Trade shows are important promotional events. Research shows that over 80 percent of trade show visitors are classified as "buying influencers" and that the typical exhibitor contacts four to five potential purchasers per hour on the show floor.[8] Trade shows also have the following benefits:

- They are an effective and efficient way to promote the company and its products to a large and interested audience.
- Decision makers and influencers can get first-hand product experience in an interpersonal setting.
- The show introduces new products to a large audience.
- Marketing and sales personnel can follow up on the qualified contacts made at the trade show. Research points to higher sales productivity in follow-up sales efforts when the customer has already been exposed to the company's products at a trade show.[9]
- The company receives high-level exposure, resulting in enhanced brand equity in the marketplace.
- The cost per contact at trade shows is significantly less than the cost of making a personal sales call.
- The show provides a chance for manufacturers, distributors, and customers to socialize in ways that may not be possible in the course of normal business relationships. (At one medical device trade show, company representatives participated in a dodgeball competition. The association hired an actor from the movie *Dodgeball: A True Underdog Story* to referee the games, and the players wore 1970s gym attire. For years after, participants continued talking about the event.)

---

[8] Ducante, D. "The Future of the United States Exhibition Industry – Flourish or Flounder, at http://www.ceir.org, October 2002.
[9] Smith, T. M., Gopalakrishna, S. and Smith, P. M. (2004), "The Complementary Effect of Trade Shows on Personal Selling," *International Journal of Research in Marketing,* 21(March), 61-69.

To benefit fully from trade show opportunities, companies must plan their event strategy well before the show begins. They should schedule appointments with customers and prospects in advance, to maximize their time at the show. Managing customer visits is also important. Trade show presentations by salespeople are significantly different from B2B sales calls. The salesperson may have only 5 to 10 minutes to make a presentation about a complex product. Instead of beginning by building rapport, and discussing their company before they present their product, salespeople at a trade show should reverse the process and start with the product. There may be no time for other niceties. They should also gather all product information in an electronic format as soon as possible after each interaction. The information will be fresh in the minds of the salespeople and easily transmitted to headquarters for timely follow up.

Companies should use a return on investment analysis to evaluate their financial investment in trade shows. As with other promotional expenditures, trade show budgeting and planning should focus on specific outcomes and objectives. Once managers establish the objectives, they should carefully evaluate all trade show expenses in terms of the number of customers attracted to a booth, the number of contacts made, and the number converted into sales.[10] The payoff from trade shows can be a sustainable competitive advantage for both manufacturers and distributors and lead to stronger relationships and newer ways to generate revenues.

---

[10] Gopalakrishna, S. and Lilien, G. L. (1993), "A Three-Stage Model of Industrial Trade Show Performance," *Marketing Science*, 14 (Winter), 22-42.

Made in the USA
Columbia, SC
09 March 2020